Praise for Anna Samios & Kickass Cashflow

"In my first business at age 20 it was drilled into me that cashflow was the 'oxygen of corporate life' so since then I always tracked cashflow before revenue and profits – the lesson served me well in Morgan & Banks, Talent2 and all my subsequent investments, as it was positive cashflow that got me through downturns and allowed us to beat the competition! This book is the best practical template of how to get it right in any business scenario!"

— Andrew Banks, Co-founder Morgan & Banks, Founder Talent2 International, Shark on TV series *Shark Tank*

"Only a business coach and business builder with the credentials of Anna Samios could create a book that's a must read for aspirational enterprise owners who want to embrace success by avoiding the number one threat to start-up and fast growing ventures – cashflow crises!"

— Peter Switzer, Director Switzer Group

"A healthy business generates cash. Cash never lies. Cash provides options for any owner or executive. Written in plain language, *Kickass Cashflow* is a book with practical tips that can be implemented immediately, that will improve your cash balance."

— David Allen, CFO Asset Management, The Agency

"I've managed businesses for over 25 years, but I [wanted] to reset and better support my finance and mortgage clients. I'm so glad I did. Anna dials straight into what matters in business, and I walked away with clear, practical actions I can apply immediately. Highly recommend for anyone serious about sustainable growth."

— Adam Buckley, Infinity Finance Solution

"We were promised tangible, practical steps we could implement right away, and that's exactly what we've received. [It] has opened my mind and helped me apply smarter strategies directly to my business. Anna's insights have shown me better ways to scale and avoid costly mistakes."

— Sarah Skinner, SLS Insurance Solutions

"Being a CEO can be lonely, but having an external advisor … when you need guidance makes a huge difference. It builds your confidence and gives you the support to make better decisions."

— Mark Hendry, CEO CIP Constructions

"The results were immediate, with noticeable improvements in team performance and revenue growth."

— Daniel McDouall, CEO Squizify

"Anna has been outstanding. She makes everything really clear, keeps it exciting and has a really good plan to execute."

— Matt Lahood, CEO The Agency Real Estate

"Anna's able to bring all different facets of commerce into the room."

— Matt Faint, Managing Director Cardionexus

How to Build a Cash-Rich Business in 30 Days

KICK ASS CASH FLOW

Anna Samios

Foreword by Verne Harnish, Bestselling Author of *Scaling Up*

Published by Performance 7
www.performance7.global
The moral right of the author has been asserted.

For quantity sales or media enquiries, please contact the publisher at the website address above.

ISBN: 978-1-7643584-0-8 (hardback)
978-1-7643584-1-5 (paperback)
978-1-7643584-2-2 (ebook)
978-1-7643584-3-9 (audiobook)

Editing by Wes Cowley and Elaine Pofeldt
Cover Design by Miladinka Milic
Typesetting by Julie Springer
Publishing Consultant Linda Diggle

Disclaimer: Although the author and publisher have made every effort to ensure the information in this book was correct at press time, the author and publisher do not assume and hereby disclaim any liability to any party for any loss, damage, or disruption caused by errors or omissions, whether such errors or omissions result from negligence, accident, or any other cause.

The author of this book does not dispense financial advice. The material in this publication is of the nature of general comment only, and does not represent professional financial (or other) advice. It is not designed to provide specific guidance for particular circumstances and it should not take the place of advice from a qualified professional. Readers should obtain professional advice where appropriate, before making any such decision. To the maximum extent permitted by law, the author and publisher disclaim all responsibility and liability (financial or otherwise) to any person, arising directly or indirectly from any person taking or not taking action based on the information in this publication.

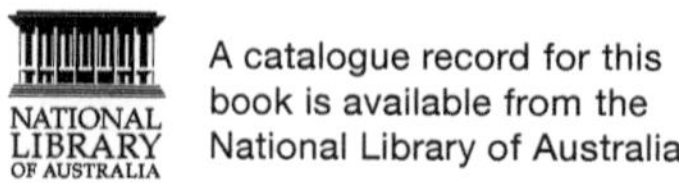

A catalogue record for this book is available from the National Library of Australia

To George, gone too soon.
A cashflow genius who found great joy
in training others in financial literacy.
We miss you every, single, day.

Gratitude

Thank you to my husband Peter, a brilliant accounting mind, who gains so much joy from sharing his deep knowledge in simple terms with business owners who are having a go!

To my children, Nathan, Jenna, and Nicholas. You have always supported me, no matter which way my creative, curious, and ambitious mind takes me.

Thank you to my parents, who kissed the word "hope" on my forehead, showered me with abundant, unconditional love, and instilled the spirit of fearlessness in my soul. "Go for it!"

Thank you to God who continues to shine light on our paths.

Contents

SECTION 2
Know the Math or Feel the Burn LTVC > CAC

SECTION 3
Growth Sucks Cash: Don't Let Ego Run the Show

SECTION 4
The WC Buckets

SECTION 5
Building Your Kickass Cashflow Team

SECTION 6
Let's Turn On Those High Beams

SECTION 7
It's Time to Kickass Your Cashflow

Foreword

Cash is the oxygen that fuels growth in any business – and you can't scale up without it. Growth "sucks cash", and if you don't have *consistent* sources of cash, ideally generated internally by your company, your business won't survive – you'll "grow broke". That is why Cash is one of the Four Decisions every company must get right, with the others being People, Strategy, and Execution.

Many leaders understand the power of cash, yet they live with the dread that they're falling behind on this crucial aspect of their business. In *Kickass Cashflow: How to Build a Cash-Rich Business in 30 Days,* Scaling Up Certified Coach Anna Samios offers an essential guide that teaches you everything you need to know to keep cash flowing into your coffers and avoid running out of it as your business grows. Even better, it will give you peace of mind, so you never have to live with the gnawing sense that you're one missed sale or uncollected account away from disaster.

In the pages to come, Anna shares what she and her team have imparted to the hundreds of mid-size businesses they've coached on Scaling Up, using colourful examples like selling Lamborghinis. You'll master concepts like Gross Margin Dollars – what's left in your pocket after generating a sale – so you never have to wonder if your business is as healthy as you think it is.

Anna will guide you through lessons on how pricing powers cashflow, the true cost of each new hire, the best way to attract sales leads that "stay and pay", how the timing of sales can make or break your business, the ideal methods to get slow payers to settle up, why every business needs a "Cashinator" to keep cash flowing smoothly, and how to forecast your cashflow with greater precision.

Kickass Cashflow is also the first book to drive home the point that cash isn't just fuel for your scale-up – it's oxygen for your nervous system. With better cashflow, you'll sleep better and age more slowly.

Devote 15 minutes a day for the next 30 days to learning the lessons she shares, and you'll know everything you need to walk into your next team huddle with the confidence that you can pay your bills, your company is secure, and you can come up with the cash to scale your business to new heights.

Cash has never been more critical to a business than it is today. *Kickass Cashflow* is the book every leader needs in order to stay on top of it. If you intend to scale, make sure this book is at the top of your reading list.

Verne Harnish
Founder of Scaling Up and the Entrepreneurs' Organization
Author of *Start to Scale* and *Scaling Up*

A Word About the Tone of This Book

By implementing the tips and tools in this book, your business can become a cash cow, allowing you to pay for all your family's expenses and live a great life.

I've been cash-strapped and cash-abundant, and having lots of cash is way better.

I'll get straight to the point and won't beat around the bush because all our business owners have families to feed. My tone may read a bit "matter of fact" and direct, and I invite you to embrace it, grab the concepts we'll be discussing, and implement them in your business, starting today. My tone is also quite conversational. As you get to know me, you'll discover that I love learning and discussing business excellence as well as how businesses can achieve peak performance.

I've written this book with the hope of introducing and reinforcing key cash concepts so that you and your business can flourish. When you have cash in your coffers, you will be calm and relaxed. When you have abundant cash and cashflow, it proves that your business is worthy of existing. It underpins the value of what you've built and gives you the freedom to fund your own growth, without bowing to banks or handing equity to external partners.

Cash brings confidence and oxygen to your thinking. It gives you time to think, to consider opportunities and weather storms.

I hope that you will take these concepts, implement them, and sleep well at night. I hope you can be physically and mentally present with your family and friends and not absent, worrying about how you're going to pay the bills and meet payroll and your tax obligations.

Ultimately, the Holy Grail in having a business that generates kickass cashflow is that you are in control. Kickass cashflow also grants you the ultimate competitive advantage: You are free to create and innovate. You are calm, can see gaps in the market, and have funds to go ahead and seize those opportunities. Kickass cashflow allows you to breathe and dream. And that's when businesses and your family truly start to flourish.

You took the leap. You backed yourself. You jumped, and that takes guts. In my world, that means you've earned the right to build the business you dreamed of: one that pays you properly, gives you freedom, and funds the incredible life you're here to live.

And here's the bonus: when the day comes that you're ready to sell, buyers will always pay more for a cashflow-positive business than for one that's a cash muncher. Cashflow isn't just your ticket to freedom today, it's your bargaining power tomorrow.

So, when my tone comes across a bit blunt, know that it comes from a place of love for privately held business and the entrepreneurial spirit.

Who this book is for:

- Anyone who started a business who wants to "have a go!"
- Owner-operated, privately held family businesses that want to grow profitably
- Companies that want to scale and hold onto their businesses so that they can one day become industry champions
- Small and medium companies that have achieved product-market fit, typically operating for more than three years (i.e., you're not a start-up)
- Companies with a headcount greater than 15 (i.e., you're not a one-man band and you have leverage)

Who this book has *not* been written for:

- Companies whose valuations are not built on profit-based metrics (e.g., some software companies with valuations based on data)
- Business owners who prefer to distort the numbers, so they don't know the truth of how their business is performing
- Owners who are addicted to ripping cash out of the business because they see a big cash balance and think *all* that money is rightfully theirs

Case studies and examples

This book is full of case studies. They are all real. For many, I have changed some names and industries to "protect the innocent", as these businesses are all still trading and scaling. The mistakes and lessons the owners learned are all real. I share them so you don't have to learn the hard way, too.

This is my why:
“To lighten the load for every business owner who wants to have a go!”

My Story

Before any of this became a mission, there was a kitchen table in Sydney. Every Friday, my parents and I sat around it, bills spread out, typewriter ready, invoice books open, sleeves rolled up and ready to go.

Dad owned a concrete pump and had a small crew. Every week, they applied pressure-sprayed concrete to swimming pools. He'd leave the house every morning whistling, full of hope. But by evening, he'd come home quiet, heavy with the weight of trying to make a small business work. He'd sometimes return home at the end of the day a broken man and that used to make me feel sad.

I remember watching him arrive home and thinking, "*What is this thing called business doing to my Dad?*" That's where it all started. Not in a boardroom, but at a kitchen table soaked in sacrifice, stress, hard work, big dreams, and love for your family.

Fast forward a generation, and I found myself at another kitchen table. This time, I sat with my husband Pete, with our first child underfoot, a mortgage hanging over our heads, and a suburban accounting practice we had begun. Cashflow was tight. Payroll was personal. Growth came in hard-fought inches. I would rush through feeding Nathan just to get back to work, juggling paperwork late into the night.

I wrote this book because one business memory haunts me more than any other. Peter and I started our first business just five months after we married. Our logic at the time was that we were working ridiculously long hours for corporate and still couldn't afford to buy a house, let alone have children. We figured that we may as well go out on our own knowing that the harder we worked, the more money we would make. Yet nothing could have been further from the truth. Whilst we were always profitable and paid loads of tax, cash was always tight.

We had our first baby, bought our first home with a $10,000 deposit, and the rest was debt. I went back to work five months later. One cold winter's evening, I ran to the supermarket to pick up a few items, including nappies for our baby. And at the checkout, I realised I didn't have enough cash to pay. Standing at that checkout, I had never felt so lonely, lost, and defeated. I had to leave the groceries and the nappies at the counter and walk away. I cannot tell you how hard it is to even revisit that memory… I tried to stay optimistic, and knew if I asked my mum for $50, she would have given it to me to buy the nappies, but I couldn't find myself to do it. It was by far one of the lowest points in my life. There I was, a hard-working, multitasking super mum, owning a business and raising a family, and we had just moved into our first home. Yet I had no cash.

The same stresses that weighed on my Mum and Dad all those years ago were now weighing on me and Peter. And our child, watching us from the kitchen table, became a mirror of my younger self, witnessing two overworked and exhausted parents doing their best to hold it all together in the name of this thing called *business*.

So, I made a decision: I set out to find the answers. Pete and I travelled to the University of New England in Australia. We immersed ourselves in a four-day offsite learning from one of the greatest minds in supporting professional service firms, Andrew Geddes. We brought everything back that we had learned, and we began working hard on the business, implementing everything he had taught us. And we successfully scaled and sold the accounting practice, which we ran for over 25 years.

Obsessed with the knowledge and ability I had to grow, scale, and exit businesses, and with Andrew's encouragement, I travelled to the US and became a Scaling Up Certified Coach, the first female coach in Australasia. I brought everything I learned back home and was soon contracted by the Australian Federal Government as a business adviser to their Entrepreneurs' Program. My expertise is in SaaS, cyber, digital and service firms and I worked with many eligible businesses to help them scale. A few years later the entrepreneurial spirit bit me again and I founded Performance 7, a boutique advisory firm specialising in scaling high-growth Australian businesses. I started the firm with one mission: **to lighten the load for every business owner who is willing to give it a go**.

Over the past three decades, I've advised over 500 companies, including university startups, multigenerational family businesses and publicly listed companies. Today, I'm a trusted adviser to the *Australian Financial Review (AFR)* Fast Growth CEOs and Chairs, as well as *AFR* Young Rich Listers. As of June 2025, Performance 7 supports a thriving portfolio of clients generating a combined $1.8 billion in annual revenue. And this figure is climbing every single day. I love the work we do to support fast-growing Aussie businesses.

Now for the full circle moment: Two of my three children, Nathan and Jenna, work alongside me at Performance 7. They bring their ideas, energy, and passion to the table. What began with my parents' struggle has become a legacy of strength and empowerment across three generations.

So why did I write *Kickass Cashflow: How to Build a Cash-Rich Business in 30 Days*?

Because I know how hard business can be, and I know it doesn't have to be that way. What you're holding in your hand or listening to is the culmination of everything I've lived and learned: the wins, the setbacks, the trial and error, and the proven strategies that work.

It's not a textbook.

It's not theory.

It's a real-world guide.

Born out of experience, designed to help you take control of your cashflow and build a business that works for *you* and not the other way around.

And here's something else: *I'm not an accountant. And that's one of my greatest strengths.* I wasn't qualified in accounting; I had to learn it the hard way. That meant cutting through the noise, stripping away the jargon, and focusing only on what matters most. I've sat in thousands of boardroom meetings, and I can tell you this: when a business owner truly understands their cashflow, they make better decisions, move faster, and sleep better at night.

If I can master cashflow, you can, too.

This is for every family business owner who's working tirelessly and still feeling stuck, who wants to stop stressing over the bank balance and start building something strong, stable, and scalable. You don't need to be a numbers person. You just need the right tools and the right guidance. I've organised this book into a 30-day plan, so you have time to absorb each concept before you move on.

I'm so excited that you're reading my book and invite you to start building kickass cashflow for your business and your family!

Together.

Anna Samios

P.S. My son Nick asked me, "Who are you writing this book for, Mum?" I paused and thought carefully of my response. "I'm writing this book for me and Dad, for when we were young and had just started our first business. I'm also writing it for Nathan and Jenna, who are having a go and running our current businesses." And I'm writing it for business owners and leaders who are seeking cashflow excellence.

Introduction

The problems with financial lipstick that hide a cashflow crisis

Lost in translation: Pretty numbers, empty bank account

Consider this your power tool which has been built for business owners who are ready to take control of their financial destiny and harness the transformative power of effective cashflow management.

The accounting profession follows rules and has established methods for recording and reporting data. International standards govern how large companies report their figures to ensure they present a true picture of their business. That said, a significant divide exists between large companies' reporting practices, privately held businesses' tax requirements, and small business owners' information needs when making growth decisions.

Many privately held businesses rely on their bookkeepers, accounting teams, and/or tax accountants to manage their calculations and tax obligations. However, sorting data to prepare your tax lodgement requirements vastly differs from how you, as a business owner, need your financial reports to be presented to you so you can make informed business decisions in a timely manner.

Problem #1: Your P&L is lying to you

Profit and loss (P&L) statements are just opinions in time. You pick a date range, feed in whatever numbers were entered for that period, and your accounting software spits out a result. Hand that same data to ten different tax accountants, and I guarantee you'll get ten different versions (and ten different opinions) of your company's profit or loss.

Despite this, we spend countless days in the life of a business navel-gazing at the profit and loss and the budgets, trying to make sense of where things went so wrong.

The problem? You start believing that one number is *the truth*. It's not. It's a snapshot bent by assumptions, coding choices, tax law interpretation, and accounting quirks. Trusting a P&L to tell you the whole story? That's like driving your cashflow with one eye shut. And that's why I rely on cash in the bank, because cash in the bank never lies. Every other number in your financial statements or tax return is merely a snapshot in time and open to manipulation and interpretation.

Cash in the bank is the most honest business partner you'll ever have.

It will tell you instantly, and without emotion, whether your business is thriving or tanking. If you don't strip it bare and you treat that account with respect, you'll start to see the patterns.

If your balance is steadily growing over time, *after* you've paid every bill, you're winning. If it's shrinking, that's your red flag and the time for an early intervention, before your cashflow starts calling the shots for you.[1]

This book directly addresses this information gap, demystifying the financial complexities of running a business, and provides practical tools and examples that are easy to understand and apply.

---

[1] This excludes cash outflows for acquisitions and large capex purchases that may distort this view for a short period of time, but the cash should return/recover more quickly if these were good investments.

Problem #2: Revenue's up, so why are you still panicking on payday?

There is much noise surrounding sales, marketing, and revenue in the entrepreneurial space. While nothing is inherently wrong with this, it's an all-too-easy mistake to think that growing sales will lead to more cash in the bank.

When my husband and I started our first business, we too believed that the harder we worked, the more money we should make! But nothing could have been further from the truth. It took us three years to realise that chasing sales at any cost to "just win the business" was the most misguided decision we could make. Sales revenue was the wrong number to focus on. I have observed both small and large businesses making this error repeatedly.

Understanding the relationship between sales and cash in the bank (the amount you have left in your pocket at the end of the day) is a groundbreaking conversation that every business needs to have. My experience, as an entrepreneur and an adviser to hundreds of businesses, indicates that once our teams understand the significance of these different numbers and how we can influence them, our businesses can become more predictable money-making machines and begin to flourish.

There's a big difference between more sales and more cash. By reading this book, you will master the factors that make these two things so different.

Problem #3: Married to the budget, divorced from reality

Cashflow makes or breaks a business. It also makes or breaks its owners and leadership team.

Over the past three decades, I've worked with hundreds of businesses, invested in many, and founded and led two of my own. And what still astounds me is how much energy gets wasted dissecting profit and loss statements, fixating on budgets that were never achievable in the first place, and then wrestling with the emotional fallout that kind of navel-gazing creates for everyone. Your business may be profitable on paper, but if, all things being equal, the numbers in your bank account aren't growing positively, then it's more than likely a sign that your business model is in distress. On the flip side, if your closing cash-at-the-bank grows after you've paid all your bills, you know you have a happy, healthy business. And you're a happy business owner.

While profit and loss analysis and budgeting are important capabilities, rolling cashflow forecasting is the *critical* skill required to run a successful business, and very few master it.

This book has been written to demystify generating cash and forecasting cashflow so that business owners can make smart, confident business decisions about their future.

Problem #4: Subtitles, please: Why your reports feel like you're watching a foreign film

Accountants, God love them, mean well. They're trained to follow standards, tick boxes, and report things accurately. But in the process, they've created a whole new dialect of business language that most owners need a translator for.

It's not malicious. It's a set of old habits.

And it's *maddening*.

You, the business owner and ultimate decision maker, end up staring at reports that feel more like IKEA instructions in Swedish. Terms get thrown around like confetti. One minute it's revenue, then it's sales, then it's "top-line" figures… and you're left wondering if you missed a memo.

No wonder it feels overwhelming.

Same numbers. Different names. All noise.

So, before we go any further, I want to eliminate that noise. We're setting the record straight, right here, right now. One language. One set of definitions. One common understanding, so you can act faster.

Here's a quick glossary of frequently used terms

Sales = sales revenue = revenue = top line = turnover

Cost of Goods Sold (COGS) = materials and labour required to deliver a product or service

Gross Margin Dollars (GM$) = Sales minus COGS

Gross Margin % = Gross margin divided by Sales, expressed as percentage.

I'll go deeper into each in the following chapters, but for now, that's our common language.

Let's go kick ass!

SECTION 1

Your Offering

We're not kicking off where you think we are.

Most people jump straight into the numbers when they hear "cashflow". But not me. I look at it differently, and I'm not afraid to say so. There are a few core fundamentals most business owners and even many advisers completely overlook when it comes to creating real, lasting cashflow. And that's exactly where we're going to start.

This section is all about building a rock-solid business model that pumps out free cashflow, not just looks good on paper.

We're not diving into bank loans, asset financing hacks, or how to charm a venture capitalist. And I'm not here to glamorise debt or capital raising either. That might be someone else's playbook, but not mine.

My priority? Helping you build a cashflow-positive business that funds its own growth. One that doesn't rely on maxed-out credit cards, second mortgages, or giving away chunks of your company just to stay afloat. You and your family deserve better than that.

This is about building a business with real strength, grounded in cash fundamentals and powered by profitable, cashflow-positive growth. My hope? That you take what's here, apply it with courage, and bootstrap your way to millions. Maybe even billions. Like many of my clients already have.

In this first section, we're going to go slow, so that later we can go fast.

You've got this.

Anna x

DAY 1

Cashflow is Oxygen: It's the Breath Behind Brilliance

There's something powerful about calm energy. It's rare and magnetic. That's why I've always loved working with Paul Stovell, co-founder and CEO of Octopus Deploy.

Paul and his wife Sonia bootstrapped their business, turning it into a serious tech success story. While Paul focused on building the team and driving product innovation, Sonia was the steady hand on the financial tiller, keeping a laser focus on cash outflows and ensuring the business stayed profitable and cashflow positive through every growth stage. By working closely together and playing to their individual strengths, they built not just a business, but a powerhouse. Together, they recently sold a minority stake to Insight Partners for a cool USD172.5 million. But here's the thing, you'd never guess the scale of what he's carrying. He's calm. Grounded. Fully present.

His secret? He knows his numbers. Paul and his team are laser-focused on how their decisions will impact cashflow. And he's built a strategic plan around that clarity. So, when challenges come, and they always do, he doesn't flinch. He leads with confidence, not chaos. That calm presence radiates through the company.

The result? A deeply loyal team. A culture built on trust. Long-term people who love working alongside each other because they feel safe. And when people feel safe, they do their life's best work. That's not fluff; that's cashflow confidence in action. Strong cashflow creates safety. Safety builds culture. And culture powers performance.

But not every business has that kind of safety net. For every leader with a loyal, thriving team, there's another quietly holding it together with duct tape and grit. The opposite of cashflow confidence is a constant undercurrent of stress, where decisions are made from fear, not strategy, and every bill feels like a ticking clock. I've seen it too many times.

Enter Melanie.

Melanie is a firecracker. Smart, fiercely loyal to her team, and running a high-performing trade business with her husband. When she first came to me, she and her husband were making millions in sales. They had scaled rapidly, but their profitability and cashflow were a mess.

Every Friday, they were shuffling invoices and bills around. They even jokingly called out "It's time to do the shuffle." Melanie would check the bank balance and have a panic attack. Her husband would try to juggle suppliers with one hand and manage their apprentices with the other. They were working 70-hour weeks and paying themselves last, if at all.

Melanie was burnt out. But more than that, she was anxious. She wasn't sleeping. She was second-guessing every business decision. Her self-worth was tanking. And the worst part? She thought it was all her fault. She thought she just wasn't "good with money". Fortunately, it was possible for Melanie and her husband to come full circle… to the calm and in control space where Paul lives every day. And it didn't involve therapy.

It was about doing what I'm about to share with you in this book: **Taking control of cashflow.**

We started with small moves. Sorted the pricing and product mix, found the money leaks, then plugged them.

Three months later, when we sat down to update the company's One-Page Strategic Plan with fresh numbers, Melanie walked into the conference room a different woman. She was standing taller. Smiling more. Her face had colour in it again. She was sleeping through the night. She had booked a long weekend with her husband and kids. She even had the bandwidth to start chatting with a software company that would help her build an online scheduling tool she'd been dreaming about for years.

Why?

Because her cashflow was under control.

Because her nervous system was no longer in fight-or-flight.

Because she finally had space to think and dream.

That's what happens when you clean up the money story. You don't just "fix the finances". You heal your relationship with yourself so you can do your own life's best work in leading your company.

Remember that moment, you know that quiet, private one you had when you picked this book up? That gut-level tug that whispered, "There's got to be a better way." Maybe you were in your office staring at a spreadsheet that didn't make sense. Maybe you were lying awake at 2 a.m., running payroll numbers in your head, wondering how on earth you were going to make it through another month. Or maybe you were smiling at your team in the morning and crying in your car that afternoon, because no one gets how hard it is to carry this.

That moment? That was real. And it was heavy.

And this is the moment it all changes. I invite you to leave it all behind. Draw a line in the sand, jump over it, and move forward. What has happened in the past, is just that: "past". What we are going to do next is all that matters. And this is where it begins. It's not just about having more money in the bank, it's about clarity in your thoughts, room to breathe in your life, and a quiet strength that settles deep within your soul. That's what positive cashflow gives you.

It's not just numbers on a page. It's oxygen for your nervous system. It's confidence in your decisions. It's the quiet power of kicking off your Monday morning knowing your bills are paid, your team is secure, and you can breathe.

I'm going to walk alongside you through the 30-day plan I've laid out in the pages ahead. These have been designed to help you find the same sense of peace and steady confidence that Paul and Melanie now feel as they continue to grow their businesses on solid ground.

Commit to reading one chapter a day for the next 30 days, and you will not only have a better understanding of the financial levers that power your company but also know all it takes to achieve the tranquillity that eludes most entrepreneurs as they take their companies to new heights.

Cashflow isn't just a business metric. It's a mental health strategy.

People think cashflow is about money. And, of course, it is.

But for business owners, especially family business owners, positive cashflow is about so much more than revenue minus expenses and chasing overdue invoices. It's about what happens inside your head, heart, and soul when the financial pressure finally lifts.

It's not just "I can pay the bills."

It's "I'm not panicking when the email pings."

It's "I'm not snapping at my kids or partner because I'm exhausted from pretending everything's fine."

It's "I'm not ashamed to look at the numbers anymore."

Money stress is one of the most corrosive forces in the human experience. It impacts family dynamics, personal relationships, and your own identity. But positive, consistent, clean cashflow is a game-changer. It doesn't just fix your business. It gives you your life back.

It's why cashflow and mental health are inseparable.

Let's talk about science for a minute.

When you're under chronic financial pressure, your body responds the same way it would to a physical threat. Your brain doesn't know the difference between a sabre-toothed tiger and a $200,000 tax bill. It just sees danger.

So, what does it do?

It floods your system with cortisol and adrenaline. You go into survival mode. You stop sleeping deeply. Your digestion suffers. Your short-term memory fades. Your creative thinking shuts down. You get irritable. You snap. You numb out. You spiral.

And then, because your thinking brain is now offline, you make dumb and dumber decisions. You miss deadlines. You underquote. You overhire. You say yes when you should say no. You become reactive instead of strategic. And the cycle repeats.

Cashflow is oxygen. Without it, your business brain shuts down.

This is why cashflow matters. Not just to your bottom line, but to your brain. When you stabilise your cashflow, you stabilise your hormones. You give your nervous system a chance to calm down. You reclaim your ability to think, lead effectively, and live peacefully.

You go from reactive to responsive. From chaos to clarity.

When you can *see* that you have created a cashflow-positive business, you show up differently. You walk into meetings with presence. You lead your team with confidence. You stop chasing every sale like your future depends on it, because deep down you know you've built something solid, something that runs with purpose and strength, even when you're not watching.

That shift to being steady, repeatable, and built from the inside out is what unlocks real happiness, control, and freedom. And it all begins when cashflow stops being a source of stress and starts becoming a source of strength.

Mark today on your calendar as the first day of your journey toward that goal.

Kickass Cashflow Power Move #1

Make a promise to yourself that you will read one chapter of this book a day and act on it with your team.

“Sales numbers are for dinner parties and margins are for boardrooms.”

— Jamie Miller, Co-CEO, WV Technologies

DAY 2

Jaws of Margin: Your Rocket Fuel

If you only read one chapter in this book, make it this one.

Getting your head around Gross Margin Dollars and how it shapes your cashflow is a total game-changer. This is the stuff that sets great businesses apart. Once you understand it, *everything* starts to click.

Gross Margin Dollars is your forward domino and where cash is born in every business.

Your go-to-market team (your marketing and sales crew) become sharper, more aligned, and far more powerful. They'll know exactly why one type of deal drives the business forward while another quietly drains your resources. No more chasing revenue for the sake of it.

You'll start having clearer, more strategic conversations about where your business is really headed and what's worth saying yes to. Your team will finally understand how pricing, discounting, and volume all work together and why gross margin isn't just a number, it's the muscle that powers your cashflow and funds your future.

In simple terms, Gross Margin Dollars is what's left in your business after you deliver a sale. It's the fuel that determines whether your business can sustain itself and has the capacity to grow. On the surface, the concept seems straightforward, almost too simple, but I see businesses of every size stumble over it every single day.

While generating sales is the lifeblood of any business, Gross Margin Dollars is the true measure of how healthy a business model is.

Many business owners, me included back in my rookie years, start out obsessed with driving sales. The logic feels sound: The harder you work, the more you sell, and the more successful you'll be. But that mindset can quickly spiral into chasing sales at any cost, which usually means razor-thin margins or even losses. The real issue is a fundamental misunderstanding between sales and gross margin, and that confusion is one of the biggest culprits behind poor cashflow. Put simply, it's energy poured into the wrong things.

When I started working with Danrae Group, it had suffered a near-death experience.

The company, based in New South Wales, Australia, provides waterproofing and remedial building solutions to the construction and property management industries.

"We almost went broke," recalls CEO Daniel Caruana, whose parents started the company 20 years ago. "The problem was we were running out of cash."

To help him understand the reason, I asked him a question that immediately pops into my mind when I start working with a scale-up whose growth is challenged: Where is the cash in the company?

As it turned out, the 80-20 rule was kicking in: About 20% of the customers were returning 80% of its total Gross Margin Dollars. And its most profitable type of work was waterproofing and remediation. Danrae needed to phase out projects in other niches that were less profitable. At one point, we calculated that its marketing + sales team costs were greater than the gross margin of the actual jobs. Ouch!

Everything shifted when they realised they were spending more money on winning new customers than they were receiving back upon delivering the sale. To emphasise how serious the company was about serving its customers, the leadership team created a Brand Promise guarantee: a "no leaks" guarantee, adding long-term maintenance to the contracts as well.

As Daniel and his leadership team kept looking to grow by winning more of their ideal customers, they still had to contend with slow cashflow. One first step to turning things around and accelerating growth was adding a clause to contracts requiring deposits. Danrae began forecasting its cashflow runway, determining how many days it could run without any income. To increase that number, it stepped up the pace of invoicing and modified its contracts to claim on them at the end of the month and mid-month, making sure that if, for instance, it paid team members weekly that it was getting paid at around the same pace.

That was seven years ago. As a result of the work we did, sales grew from about $1.5 million, with 18 employees, to nearly $10 million, with 30 team members. The company's cash in the bank rose to about $800,000 at any given time, up from $150,000.

When we talk about sales, we refer to the total sales revenue generated by one's business activities. It's easy to get caught up in the excitement of high sales numbers, but it's important to remember that sales alone don't paint the full picture of your business's financial health. Gross Margin Dollars, on the other hand, is what remains after you have deducted all *direct* costs from your sales. It is the true measure of your business's product-market fit and, if you maximise it, is your greatest chance at increasing your cash in the bank.

Here is a formula that will help you visualise it:

Gross Margin Dollars = Sales – Cost of Goods Sold (COGS)

COGS comprises the direct expenses you tie directly back to a specific product or service, like materials and labour. For example, in a plumbing business, the pipes and the plumber's time for a specific job are direct costs.

Indirect costs, on the other hand, are necessary to run the business but can't be traced to one customer, product, or service. These include things like warehouse and storage rent, plumbers' vehicles, utilities, and the administration team's salaries. They're costs that support the entire business, not just one job.

Direct Costs	**Indirect Costs**
Materials for a specific job (e.g., pipes for a plumbing job)	Rent and outgoings
Labour directly tied to the job (e.g., plumber's wages for a specific repair)	Utilities (electricity, water, etc.)
Raw materials (for product-based businesses)	Administrative salaries (office team, managers)
Cost of subcontractors for a particular project	Insurance
Packaging for a specific product	Office expenses
Items purchased for resale	Sales and marketing
Travel costs related to a specific job or project (e.g., airfares, accommodation, meals, etc.)	Accounting and legal fees

Table 1: Direct vs. Indirect Costs

Lamborghini exercise

Every time I keynote, there's one exercise people never forget – the Lamborghini exercise. I came up with it on the fly one day while facilitating a leadership team meeting. This team was caught in a dangerous loop: obsessively discounting to win more business. They thought shaving a little off the price was harmless. What they didn't see was how much money they were leaving on the table, or how hard they'd have to work to replace it. The Lamborghini exercise changed their perspective in minutes.

Let's walk through this easy example that demonstrates how understanding Gross Margin Dollars can help you grow your business. You can use Table 2 as a reference to guide you.

You wake up one morning, see an opportunity in the market to sell Lamborghinis, and decide to set up shop. Congratulations: You're running a start-up!

You sell one Lamborghini for $1,000,000, so now your total sales is $1,000,000. You pay the supplier $700,000, freight $50,000, and yourself as the salesperson[2] $100,000. You're left with a gross margin of $150,000 (See Table 2).

Now, you think to yourself, "This business has legs... let's scale!"

The scale-up

Your new business is off to a healthy start. You sell 10 Lamborghinis at $1 million each. Total sales $10 million. You pay the supplier $7,000,000 for the cars and the freight company $500,000. You keep your salary at $100,000 for a full year's work. Your Gross Margin Dollars are $2.4 million (See Table 2).

---

[2] We've included the salesperson in direct labour because, in this case, the business is all about selling cars. If you prefer, you may exclude the salesperson's salary in your calculations. The message will not change. Margin dollars multiplied by volume = potential to scale.

Lamborghini Exercise

Decision	Start Up	Scale Up	10% Discount	10% Price Increase	10% Price & 50% Qty Increase
Quantity	1	10	10	10	15
Price $	1,000,000	1,000,000	900,000	1,100,000	1,100,000
Sales Revenue $	1,000,000	10,000,000	9,000,000	11,000,000	16,500,000
Pay manufacturer $	(700,000)	(7,000,000)	(7,000,000)	(7,000,000)	(10,500,000)
Pay Freight $	(50,000)	(500,000)	(500,000)	(500,000)	(750,000)
Pay Direct Labour $ (salesperson)	(100,000)	(100,000)	(100,000)	(100,000)	(150,000)
Gross Margin $	$150,000	$2,400,000	$1,400,000	$3,400,000	$5,100,000

Table 2: Lamborghini exercise

Discount Donna

It's happy days… but you get a bit bored and need a new challenge. You get distracted by a new big idea and reach out to an old friend, Donna, whom you decide to hire as a salesperson. She says, "Ten cars?! Piece of cake… no worries." After a few weeks, she says, "I can make these cars fly out the door. All I have to do is discount them by 10% and make it up in volume – too easy."

Sounds simple, but let's look at what that means for your business and your Gross Margin Dollars. If you sell 10 cars x $900,000 each (allowing for a 10% discount), less the $7,000,000 to the manufacturer and $500,000 to the freight company, and you pay your friend's salary, $100,000, you're left with $1.4 million profit. Donna's 10% discount just burnt a $1 million hole in your pocket. Your Gross Margin Dollars dropped by $1 million! Can you envision me collapsing on the floor?

Take a look at Table 3 on the following page to see how this seemingly small discount affects your numbers. The numbers tell us that at 25% gross margin and a discount of 10%, Donna would have to sell 67% more cars just *to make the same* Gross Margin Dollars without the price cut. In other words, she has to sell 17 cars to make the same Gross Margin

Dollars as if she hadn't discounted at all!

Read that again. Eye-watering, isn't it?

We calculated our gross margin from column 2, where we scaled up to $2.4m, divided by $10m in sales equals 24% and then used the table below to calculate the volume increase that Donna would need to get gross margin back to $2.4m.

		If your present margin is:								
		20%	25%	30%	35%	40%	45%	50%	55%	60%
And		To produce the same profit your sales volume must increase by:								
you	2%	[illegible]	[illegible]	[illegible]	[illegible]	[illegible]	[illegible]	[illegible]	[illegible]	[illegible]
reduce	4%	[illegible]	[illegible]	[illegible]	[illegible]	[illegible]	[illegible]	[illegible]	[illegible]	[illegible]
your	6%	[illegible]	[illegible]	[illegible]	[illegible]	[illegible]	[illegible]	[illegible]	[illegible]	[illegible]
price	8%	[illegible]	[illegible]	[illegible]	[illegible]	[illegible]	[illegible]	[illegible]	[illegible]	[illegible]
by:	10%	100%	67%	50%	[illegible]	[illegible]	[illegible]	[illegible]	[illegible]	[illegible]
	12%	[illegible]	[illegible]	[illegible]	[illegible]	[illegible]	[illegible]	[illegible]	[illegible]	[illegible]
	14%	[illegible]	[illegible]	[illegible]	[illegible]	[illegible]	[illegible]	[illegible]	[illegible]	[illegible]
	16%	[illegible]	[illegible]	[illegible]	[illegible]	[illegible]	[illegible]	[illegible]	[illegible]	[illegible]
	18%	[illegible]	[illegible]	[illegible]	[illegible]	[illegible]	[illegible]	[illegible]	[illegible]	[illegible]
	20%	[illegible]	[illegible]	[illegible]	[illegible]	[illegible]	[illegible]	[illegible]	[illegible]	[illegible]
	25%	[illegible]	[illegible]	[illegible]	[illegible]	[illegible]	[illegible]	[illegible]	[illegible]	[illegible]
	30%	[illegible]	[illegible]	[illegible]	[illegible]	[illegible]	[illegible]	[illegible]	[illegible]	[illegible]

Table 3: Discounting table

For a detailed view of this discounting table go to:
www.KickassCashflow.com

> **BUSINESS OWNER'S TIP:**
> I was lucky to discover this discounting table in my twenties, and it completely changed how I thought about business strategy. I shared before that when we set up our first business, our logic was that the more sales we closed, the more money we would have in our pocket, but nothing was further from the truth. Understanding the need to focus on Gross Margin Dollars changed my business life. Now I'm sharing what I learned with you.

Pricing Princess

The adventure with Discount Donna reveals only part of the picture when it comes to pricing. What if instead of hiring her, you bumped into another friend who said "One million dollars? We should sell them at $1.1 million each. We'll find the right people who truly love the car."

You hire your friend, and she sells 10 cars at $1.1 million, bringing in $11 million in sales revenue. You pay the supplier and freight forwarder as usual, along with the Pricing Princess's salary, and come away with a whopping $3.4 million in Gross Margin Dollars! *That* is the power of pricing.

Pricing correctly is the ultimate business hack. Get your pricing right, and you're more than halfway to conquering your cash and cashflow.

Price and volume (Column 5)

If you want to seriously scale, you'll soon fall in love with *increasing both price and volume simultaneously*. The last column in Table 2 shows that with a 10% increase in price, together with a 50% increase in volume and a 50% bonus for your salesperson, you will end up with $5.1 million in Gross Margin Dollars in your pocket. This example shows the true meaning of working smarter, not harder. Dare I say, your Pricing Princess just graduated to a Kickass Cashflow Queen!

Sales team sales targets

Setting clear Gross Margin Dollars targets for your sales team can help you optimise your cashflow. Unlike sales targets focusing purely on top-line growth, Gross Margin Dollars targets align sales team efforts with your business's profitability goals and, therefore, cashflow goals. Your sales team is not just chasing revenue but is also mindful of the costs involved in generating that revenue, so their efforts contribute positively to the bottom line.

Gross margin–based targets should ideally incentivise your sales team to prioritise activities that yield the highest returns. By focusing on these high-gross-profit activities, your team can maximise the Return on Investment (ROI) for the business and minimise the time spent on less profitable deals. This shift in focus helps create a culture within your business that emphasises profitability over sheer revenue generation, leading to more sustainable growth.

In addition, the number one thing a salesperson won't ever do, in a culture like this, is default to discounting to win new business. **Discounting erodes Gross Margin Dollars. Think of it like hydrochloric acid dripping all over your invoices. It burns a hole in your business's pocket and your cashflow, too.**

Discounting isn't just a pricing problem; it's a culture problem. The moment you allow one discount for the wrong reason, you open the door for more. What starts as a one-off quickly becomes systemic. Before long, your team assumes discounting is the norm, not the exception. And that mindset quietly eats away at confidence, erodes margins, and undermines the culture you've worked so hard to build. If you allow it once, you've set the tone and your team will follow your lead straight into a race to the bottom.

If the only trick the sales team has in the bag is to pull out a discount to win the business, then, in my experience, it will be the first sign that everyone needs sales training. The only other possible reason is that the value proposition isn't compelling or competitive enough. We'll cover this in more detail in Day 11, when we discuss "the no-brainer offer".

That brings us back to our Lamborghini exercise. As a business owner, you would have been better off giving Donna a clear target based on Gross Margin Dollars, as opposed to a sales target. Donna would have been focused on the right job to be done. By giving her a clear goal, you would have set her up for success and the chance of bigger sales commissions.

If this chapter made you pause, even for a second, lean into that. Because this isn't just about numbers on a spreadsheet. It is the first step that will help you build a business that generates free cash and works *for* you, not the other way around. Understanding Gross Margin Dollars changes how you sell, price, lead, and grow. It gives you clarity, control, and confidence.

Hitting your Gross Margin Dollars targets is the *first step* toward generating real cash.

No gross margin, then no money left to pay for other expenses. This leads to no net profit.

No net profit, then no chance at any cash.

It's that simple.

So, take what you've learned, shake off the old habits, and make the shift away from talking about "How many sales did we make?" to "How much Gross Margin Dollars did we generate?" Your cashflow depends on it.

The Jaws of Margin

Think of your gross margin like a set of jaws.

- The top jaw is determined by your selling price.
- The bottom jaw is your COGS (we'll cover this more in the following chapters).

When the top jaw (price) goes up, or the bottom jaw (COGS) goes down, the jaws open wider. But start discounting or letting costs creep up, and those jaws close in on you. If they close too far, they bite straight into your profitability and cashflow.

A few key truths:

- **Price is powerful:** A small percentage increase in price flows almost entirely to your bottom line.
- **COGS is relentless:** If it rises and you don't pass on the increase, your margin gets crushed.
- **The danger zone:** When prices are under pressure and COGS is rising, the jaws snap shut fast. And Houston… we have a problem.

We'll dig deeper into each of these concepts later, but first I want to show you a graph that makes the numbers speak. When you plot sales and

COGS over time, the gap between the two lines becomes your "Jaws of Margin". It's one of the most powerful visuals you'll ever use to understand and protect your profitability.

At Performance 7, we know that a company's strategy is right if the Jaws of Margin are widening (See Figure 1). In fact, one of our clients, let's call him Gary, recently announced during their leadership team offsite, "Anna, I don't just want Jaws of Margins, I want us to be a Shark!"

So, here's our rule: If the **Jaws of GM$** are widening, then your strategy is winning. Full stop. That's our bulletproof test. A data-backed, no-nonsense way to know if your gut feeling is right, if your sales team is on the right track, and if we have any chance of building cash at bank.

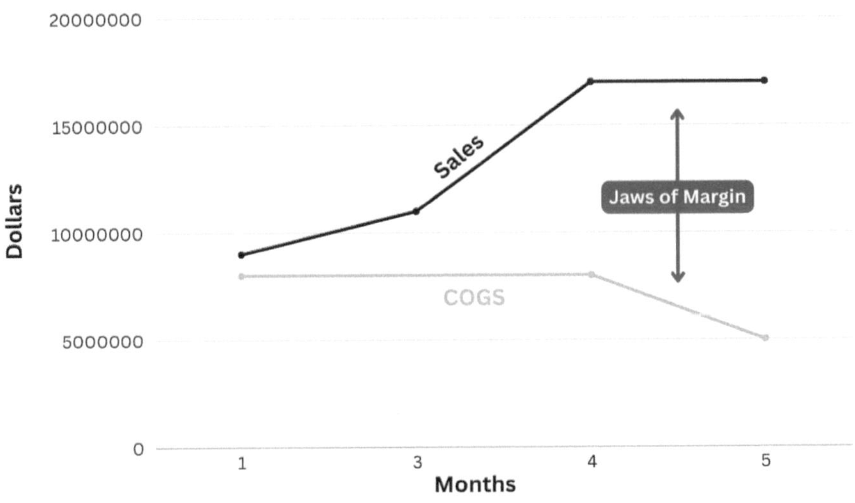

Figure 1: Jaws of Margin

Kickass Cashflow Power Move #2

Stop being mesmerised by big sales numbers. Calculate the Gross Margin Dollars numbers. That is your first step to build cashflow that sticks.

DAY 3

Pricing Powers Cashflow

Pricing is the gift that keeps on giving.

Let's go deeper into this real power move: pricing. When you get this right, everything changes.

If you want to build momentum, drive serious Gross Margin Dollars, and take the reins on your cashflow, I encourage you to start here. Pricing is often dismissed as a small tweak, but it's not. It's the most powerful lever in your business. And the best part? You control it. No banks, no approvals, no outside permission. Just one bold decision at a time.

This is where things start to shift, and you deserve to understand it fully. Increasing your prices fairly and strategically is one of the fastest, most effective ways to create positive cashflow. Most people don't do it because they're, understandably, afraid. Fearful they'll lose customers. Worried people will say no. Afraid they're not worth it. But here's the truth: Smart pricing has nothing to do with greed. It's about sustainability. It's about building a business that can breathe, grow, and look after its people.

This is a cashflow tactic that our Pricing Princess clearly understood in Day 2's Lamborghini example. A price increase increases the sales number, and the improvement in dollars drops straight to the bottom line. It doesn't even touch the sides; it goes directly into your business's pocket. Like I said. Understand the power of pricing and you have just about mastered the art of Kickass Cashflow. Get it wrong and you're in a world of hyperventilation and misery.

And in today's climate, where inflation, rising costs, and cost-of-living pressures are squeezing every dollar, *getting pricing right isn't a luxury; it's a necessity.* It's not a "nice to have", or something you'll look at when things calm down. It's a *strategic muscle* you and your team need to build now, not later, if you want any chance of winning on the cashflow front.

Many avoid pricing increases as they fear they will lose business. Equally, they often have a fear of conflict and prefer to keep things the same, as in "if it ain't broke, don't fix it", but it *is* broken. Inflation and the cost of goods have increased, and your Gross Margin Dollars is being squeezed. It's time to update your price list.

Pricing is a sustainable growth strategy, not a guess

Let's start with the basics. Pricing isn't just about covering your costs and landing the sale. It's about building a business that works for you, your team, and the future you're working so hard for.

Get it right, and you'll have the cashflow to hire the right people, invest in growth, and sleep soundly at night. Get it wrong, and you'll find yourself sprinting on a treadmill that never actually moves forward.

Here's what smart pricing needs to reflect:

- **Your costs:** Everything it takes to deliver what you sell: direct costs, indirect costs, and the hidden costs people often ignore, like tax.
- **Your value:** What your product or service is truly worth in the eyes of your customer.

It also needs to support your financial goals. If you're aiming for a specific Gross Margin Dollars target, your pricing needs to deliver on that. Not eventually, but *right now.* And let's be clear: Pricing is not a "set it and forget it" kind of decision. You've got to revisit it often, just like your costs shift, your brand strengthens, and your market evolves.

But here's something just as important: **If you want to build a long-term, sustainable business, you also need to price fairly.** Price with strength, but always with integrity. Fair pricing builds trust and long-term relationships. It creates repeat customers. It fuels reputation. *Price fair. Never gouge.* The goal isn't to squeeze every dollar from every sale. It's to build a business that lasts, serves, and grows.

The two pricing models every leader should understand

There are dozens of pricing models, but two are foundational. Learn them, and you'll immediately be ahead of the pack and will be able to talk about pricing like a pro.

Cost-plus pricing

This is the simplest method. You take the total cost of producing your product or delivering your service, then add a markup. For example, if it costs you $100 to produce and you want a 30 per cent markup, your price is $130.

It's clean. It's safe. It works well in industries with stable costs and steady demand.

But here's the problem: *Cost-plus pricing doesn't account for perceived value.* It doesn't consider what your customer is willing to pay based on the benefit they receive. That means you might be leaving money on the table. And if your costs increase and your pricing doesn't adjust, you start cutting into your cashflow without even realising it.

Value-based pricing

Value-based pricing flips the model. Instead of starting with your costs, you start with your customer. What is the result they're getting from your product or service? How much time, money, or energy does it save them? What pain does it take away? That's what you're selling, and that's what should shape your price. If you're offering a service that helps someone avoid a $50,000 mistake, a $10,000 price tag is not only fair, it's generous. Value-based pricing is how you protect your Gross Margin Dollars, increase your cash reserves, and build a financially strong business.

To make this work, you need to

- know your customer deeply,
- quantify the impact you're making,
- communicate that value, and
- keep an eye on where you sit in the market.

Value-based pricing works best when your offering is unique, high quality, or niche. It puts the power back in your hands because you're no longer pricing to survive. You're pricing to grow.

Why a pricing error directly impacts cashflow

We covered this in Day 2, but it's worth covering again so that you truly understand the pain that discounting inflicts on a business. If you underprice by just 10%, the loss is not a rounding error, it's a direct hit to your gross margin. Multiply that 10% across your total sales volume and you'll quickly see how much profit is leaking out of your business every single day.

Unlike other costs, this leak is self-inflicted. You don't ever get it back. And worse, you have to work much, much harder to sell more units just to recover the lost gross margin.

Here's another simple example:

Let's say your business sells $1,000,000 worth of goods a year with a gross margin of 30%. At the correct price, you make $300,000 in gross margin – win! If you discount by 10%, sales revenue falls to $900,000, and if you have the same cost base your gross margin crashes to $200,000.

That's $100,000 gone, forever. To recover you'd have to increase your sales volume by 50% just to get back to where you were before discounting.

Here's what most people forget: The *cash that is left in your bank account doesn't come from revenue. It comes from Gross Margin Dollars.* That's why pricing matters so much. Pricing is one of the key levers you can pull to increase your cash at bank.

Let's say you underprice by just 10 per cent across the board. Multiply that by your sales volume and you'll quickly see how much money is leaking out of your business. Those missing Gross Margin Dollars? That's your ability to invest. That's your freedom. That's your cashflow: gone. Never to be seen again.

More sales can create more problems

We've all heard the advice: "Just sell more." But here's what nobody says out loud: *More sales at low Gross Margin Dollars puts enormous pressure on your delivery team.* They're forced to move faster, take shortcuts, and stretch beyond what's sustainable. Mistakes happen. Quality suffers. Customers get cranky. And the team starts to burn out.

All of this eats into your cash – the rework, mistakes, and crankiness. And Monday morning the cycle starts again.

If your product mix shifts toward lower–Gross Margin Dollars items or if you chase volume without considering the true operational cost, your business may look busy on the outside, but inside it's quietly breaking down.

That's why Gross Margin Dollars–based sales are so critical. They keep your delivery team focused, your customers happy, and your bank balance healthy.

The other side of the coin: Price increase

I get it. Raising prices can feel terrifying. It used to be terrifying to me too in the early days. The fear is real: *What if I lose all my customers? What if they go to my competitors?* But here's the kickass move most business owners don't realise: A well-calculated price increase can be one of the fastest ways to boost your cashflow without working harder. Take this example, if your gross margin is 25% and you raise your prices by 10%, you could afford to lose a full quarter of your sales revenue and still make the same Gross Margin Dollars as you did before the price rise. That's right, you could do less work, serve fewer customers, and still earn the same money. That's the quiet, untapped power of pricing.

If you'd like a copy of the pricing table behind this example, go to **KickassCashflow.com**

The guardrails: Leadership must own the pricing

I've seen companies lose millions (yes, millions!) because they handed off pricing decisions to the wrong people. Usually, it's a well-meaning sales team, desperate to close the deal, that starts discounting without understanding the ripple effect.

Pricing decisions need to rest with the people who see the whole picture: the CEO, the leadership team, and the CFO. This isn't about control. It's about protecting your Gross Margin Dollars, your cashflow, and your ability to lead from a place of confidence.

Final word: Own your value; master your future

You have more power than you realise. The price you set says everything about how you value your work and how you expect others to value it, too.

So, here's your challenge:

Review your prices.

Understand your Gross Margin Dollars.

Ask yourself if your current pricing supports the business and life you want to build.

Because price isn't just a number. *It's a decision. A strategy. A gift that keeps on giving.* And it starts today with you and your leadership team.

Kickass Cashflow Power Move #3

Be courageous and review your prices every quarter.

"Discard everything that does not spark joy."

— Marie Kondo

DAY 4

Stack, Shuffle, and Slay Your COGS

First, a truth bomb about accountants

Most accountants don't present your financials in a way that lets you instantly see your real COGS, and, honestly, it's not their fault. You hired them to keep the tax office happy, tick all the compliance boxes, and prepare tidy reports so they can hit "submit" on your GST or VAT return without drama. Their job is to allocate and group expenses for form-filling, not to give you the kind of clarity that helps you make sharper business decisions and supercharge your cashflow.

So, here's the challenge: If you're still basing your pricing, strategy, or growth moves on the COGS in the P&L that your tax agent prepared, you might as well be driving blindfolded. Stop. Let's pause, rip off the blindfold, and get the real numbers before you make your next move.

Accurate, detailed data isn't just a "nice to have", it's your competitive edge. When you can trust the numbers, you can back your decisions with confidence. You'll know exactly which products are worth doubling down on, which services are draining profit, and where every single dollar is flowing. Without that clarity, you're guessing, reacting instead of leading, and leaving your cashflow at the mercy of chance. Data turns gut feelings into grounded strategy, and in business, that's the difference between drifting and deliberately steering towards Kickass Cashflow nirvana.

Let's roll up our sleeves

As unglamorous as it might sound, knowing and calculating your true cost of goods sold is non-negotiable if you want to build real profit and cashflow. COGS is made up of **two key components**:

- **Materials:** every part, product, raw ingredient, or consumable used to deliver your offer.
- **Direct labour:** the wages, salaries, and oncosts for the people who physically make, build, ship, or perform the work for your clients.

In other words, COGS includes every *direct* cost required to deliver your product or service, such as materials, parts, freight, travel, meals, and accommodation related to delivery, and the labour it takes to get the job done. If the client would expect to pay for that material or person as part of delivering the service, it's COGS. Accurate COGS tells you the real cost of delivering the product or service.

What's not COGS? Anything that isn't directly tied to delivering the work: things like rent, your internet bill, or flights to an international conference. Those are overheads.

When you know your *true* COGS, you can finally see your real Gross Margin Dollars, and that's where every smart growth and cashflow conversation begins. But here's the catch: If your accountant's profit and loss doesn't allocate salaries and wages in the right section, your numbers are already skewed. Misplacing wages in your profit and loss is one of the biggest causes of misleading gross margin numbers. If wages aren't allocated correctly,

- your cost of goods will be wrong,
- your gross margin percentage will be distorted, and
- you'll make bad pricing decisions.

Before you start, clean up your reports yourself or get your accountant's help, so you're making decisions based on facts not fiction.

Step 1: Stack

Many business owners believe that the more rows, numbers, and data in their P&L statement the better their decision-making will be. The opposite is true.

A highly detailed P&L can overwhelm you with noise, hide the big picture, and delay decisions. Details are great for accountants doing compliance work, but it's terrible for business owners trying to run a business.

Figure 2 shows an example of the report we usually get. Rows and rows of blah, blah, blah numbers that are perfectly accurate (mostly), but do nothing to help you truly understand how to improve your business – the "so what?" is missing!

Profit and Loss
Demo Company (AU)

Account	Apr-25	May-25	Jun-25
Trading Income			
Sales	444,742	453,568	475,654
Total Trading Income	**444,742**	**453,568**	**475,654**
Cost of Sales			
Purchases	333,557	353,783	380,534
Total Cost of Sales	**333,557**	**353,783**	**380,534**
Gross Profit	**111,186**	**99,785**	**95,120**
Operating Expenses			
Advertising	4,091	1,234	1,785
Bank Fees	311	221	280
Cleaning	310	314	344
Consulting & Accounting	987	1,025	1,145
Entertainment	200	477	389
Freight & Courier	150	140	175
General Expenses	118	967	775
Legal expenses	3,994	940	1,398
Light, Power, Heating	400	645	744
Motor Vehicle Expenses	568	370	455
Office Expenses	213	1,327	985
Printing & Stationery	230	336	444
Rent	2,574	3,000	3,000
Subscriptions	120	180	140
Telephone & Internet	182	158	188
Travel - National	220	462	333
Wages and Salaries	54,522	56,789	57,555
Total Operating Expenses	**69,190**	**68,585**	**70,135**
Net Profit	**41,996**	**31,200**	**24,985**

Figure 2: Profit and Loss Statement

Figure 3 shows what we need to see.

Step 2: Shuffle

Simple Profit and Loss
Demo Company (AU)

Account	Apr-25	May-25	Jun-25
Revenue	**444,742**	**453,568**	**475,654**
COGS	333,557	353,783	380,534
Gross Profit	**111,185**	**99,785**	**95,120**
GP %	25%	22%	20%
Direct Labour (DL)	34,522	36,789	37,555
Gross Profit (After DL)	**76,663**	**62,996**	**57,565**
GP%	17%	14%	12%
Operating Expenses			
Management Admin Wages	20,000	20,000	20,000
Occupancy	2,574	3,000	3,000
Other	12,093	8,796	9,580
Total Operating Expenses	**34,667**	**31,796**	**32,580**
Operating Profit	**41,996**	**31,200**	**24,985**

Figure 3: Simple Profit and Loss Statement

This formatting of the P&L is attributed to Greg Crabtree's *Simple Numbers* book. A *Simple Numbers*–style layout cuts out all the noise and focuses your attention where it matters. When it comes to COGS, split it into two buckets:

- Direct costs excluding labour
- Direct labour costs

This simple separation tells you straight away if your problem is with materials and other costs, or with labour. If materials are creeping up, you know to look at suppliers, waste, or purchasing. If labour is too high, you know to look at your team, productivity, or efficiency. By seeing the problem clearly, you can fix the right thing fast without getting lost in a sea of numbers.

Reach out to our team if you'd like help creating these reports at:
www.KickassCashflow.com

Once you've allocated the costs to the right section of your P&L, then we can start working on improving our COGS.

Step 3: Slay

Remember the Jaws of Margin graph that we discussed in Day 2? COGS is the bottom line that we want to drop as much as possible, without sacrificing a great customer and team experience.

The COGS line is the second step to widening the Jaws of Margin.

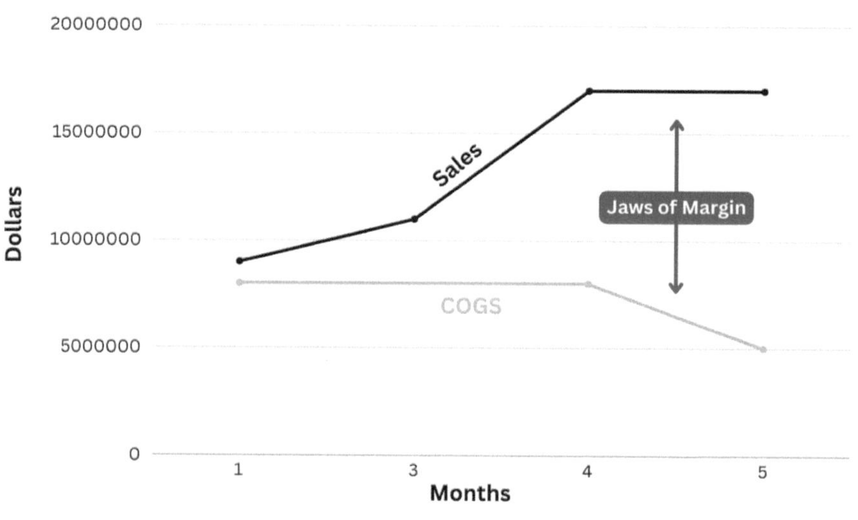

Figure 4: Jaws of Margin

Here's your friendly, but firm, word of warning: Almost every accountant I've sat across from in a boardroom has said, "You've got to cut costs if you want to improve your profit." And while technically true, it's also **dangerously one-dimensional and short-sighted** if that's where the conversation ends.

Now, I'm not saying go rogue with your COGS. Most founders I work with are already hustling hard by negotiating supplier rates, chasing rebates, managing wage structures, scheduling and squeezing what they can. But there's a fine line between being lean… and going cheap.

Don't let cost-cutting kill quality

Reducing COGS by simply cutting corners using cheaper, inferior materials or hiring low-cost, inexperienced direct labour might give you a short-term bump in gross margin, but it's a recipe for long-term damage. Quality drops, mistakes increase, rework costs rise, and your reputation suffers. Customers notice, loyalty erodes, and the very sales you rely on to cover overheads start to decline. Sustainable improvement in COGS comes from smarter purchasing, better supplier relationships, higher process efficiencies, and training your people to work faster and smarter, not from sacrificing the value your customers expect.

Cut the fat, not the value

Smart scaling means protecting the parts of your offer that build trust and keep clients coming back. That's how you create a Jaws of Margin that's not just wider but remains wider for years to come.

If you go down the quick-fix path of cutting costs to increase your Gross Margin Dollars, you need to counter-balance the argument to consider whether your client lifetime value will plummet, referrals may dry up, and you need to start spending more to win back what you lost.

That's not smart. That's sabotage.

And sabotage is very expensive.

When I worked with the Federal Government's Entrepreneurs Programme, I was constantly blown away by how much brainpower and energy management teams poured into one thing: slashing costs. For them, the Holy Grail was being better, faster, cheaper, whether or not the leaner version of what they made would even matter in the market tomorrow. Some weren't even subtle about it; it was all about scoring a fat bonus at year's end.

In their race to cut costs, they hacked away at products, services, and even entire customer segments that were already on their way out. They were so busy trimming yesterday's business that they couldn't see the goldmine sitting right under their nose.

I still see it with publicly listed companies and certain private equity–backed businesses. Executives live or die by monthly KPIs, board meetings, market announcements, and quarterly wins. The pressure to deliver short-term results and protect their bonus is relentless. It's also a dangerous trap.

Here's the edge you have as a privately held business: You're in it for the long haul. You don't have to answer to the market's mood swings. Yes, every profit gain feels good, but gutting quality or wrecking the customer experience just to shave a few dollars off the cost line? That's the slow road to irrelevance. Long-term cashflow confidence beats short-term cost-cutting glory every single time.

The real conversation should be: *Which high-GP$ products or services can we optimise first to build a sustainable competitive advantage?* That's where the long-term cashflow magic happens. Cost-cutting for the sake of cutting costs, especially in areas that will never give you a competitive edge, isn't a strategy. It's a countdown clock to becoming obsolete.

Instead, review your COGS with a fine-tooth comb and ask, "Is this providing value to the core customer, and will it give us a competitive advantage?" If yes, then keep it, but if it's not helpful, you must make a cut. Remove the emotion – it comes down to preserving every single dollar of cash.

Because...

If you want to grow with confidence, you need to know, hand on heart, your Gross Margin Dollars. No guessing, no "close enough". And here's the truth: You can't own your gross margin if you don't first know your COGS.

With well-understood and accurate COGS,

- you price with clarity,
- you quote with confidence,
- you stop guessing and start leading into new markets, and
- you can dominate.

And that's the shift from busy and broke to paid like a boss.

Kickass Cashflow Power Move #4

Get your COGS correct, and every other decision falls into line.

“Not all labour is created equal:
some fuel cashflow, some consume it.
Know the difference.”

— George Tsiamis

DAY 5

Know the Cost of a New Hire

Stellar Tech Solutions[3] is a fast-growing IT services firm whose leaders knew they needed help when they approached me. Projects were ballooning. Deadlines were slipping. Their engineers were bogged down with admin. So, they decided to hire a project manager (PM).

Now, this wasn't a knee-jerk decision. Before posting the job ad, they did the math. Salary, superannuation, benefits, onboarding, tools, and a training buffer. They mapped it all out. They asked the right question: "Will this hire help us generate more margin dollars and improve cashflow within the year?"

Their answer was yes. Their decision was based on the numbers, not on anecdotal evidence where the team were pleading for admin help because they personally found it boring.

The new PM didn't bring in cash immediately. Instead, she built the systems. Cleaned up the chaos. Freed the engineers to focus on billable work in a 100-day plan. She wasn't a revenue line yet. But by month six, Stellar Tech could take on more projects, deliver faster, and improve Gross Margin Dollars by 17%. That PM didn't just cover her cost.

[3] Whose name has been changed for anonymity.

She made herself cashflow-positive in less than five months. Revenue followed rigour. Now that's a hire with a ROI.

Hiring without watching cashflow is a rookie move

When most leaders talk about hiring, they are referring to headcount, not cost. They see a role to help take away some of the tasks and don't consider the revenue ripple. But if you want kickass cashflow, you need to know exactly what that hire is going to do for your bottom line and when.

Whether someone is revenue-generating or not, they cost your business more than their salary. Let's break it down:

- **Superannuation:** At 12%, an $80,000 salary now costs $89,600.
- **Leave loadings:** Annual leave, sick days, and public holidays reduce your effective working weeks, resulting in fewer billable hours – more hidden costs. And if they don't take their annual leave, it means you have paid them for 56 weeks of work!
- **Payroll tax and insurance:** Add 5-10%, depending on your jurisdiction and sector.
- **Recruitment, onboarding, and training:** These easily add up to 10-20% of salary. Many recruiters invoice this amount on the day the employee starts. Spending that cash before they are profitable puts you in deeper in your Valley of Death, a financial scenario where you are in imminent danger of running out of money.
- **Resources:** Desk, laptop, software, coffee, and amenities. They add up.

By the time you're done, that "$80,000 hire" could cost you $112,000 a year or more. And that's fine, *if* they're producing more value than they consume.

Margin %

Once you've calculated the total cost of hiring a new employee, the second calculation you need is your margin percentage.

Gross margin% = Gross Margin Dollars divided by Sales Dollars x 100

This tells us for each dollar of sales how much gross margin is created by the business.

A note from George: Direct vs. indirect labour

As you may have noticed, I dedicated this book to my cousin George, a brilliant CFO. He passed away during COVID and left a huge hole in our lives. He is dearly missed, even today as I write this chapter.

During COVID, George and I would spend endless hours discussing cashflow and the serious gap in cash decision training. One of the most memorable lessons he shared with me was based on his reading of Greg Crabtree's books.

Here's what George taught me: *Not all labour is created equal, especially when it comes to cashflow.*

- **Direct labour** is the team that's hands-on with your product or service: your carpenters, your team in the field, your lawyers and consultants. Their time is billable and directly tied to revenue. These costs sit in your cost of goods sold.
- **Indirect labour** is your backstage crew: admin, ops, and marketing. (It may even include you if you are not customer-facing). This team's work supports delivery but is not billable. These costs sit in overhead.

Get this wrong and your revenue targets and cashflow forecasting calculations go out the window.

Teams will often say, "We're slammed, we need more people!" Before you race to post a job ad, stop and ask the golden question George used to ask: "Is this role direct labour or indirect labour?"

For example, imagine a landscaping company in growth mode. They're weighing up whether to hire an admin assistant at $60,000 each (indirect labour) to handle the office workload or bring on another landscaper at $60,000 who can deliver more billable jobs (direct labour). The choice isn't just about who's busiest, it's about who will we hire so that we will boost cashflow fastest.

Let's look at the numbers.

The sales target formula for funding your next A-Player on the front line (direct labour)

Required Additional Revenue = Direct Labour Expense ÷ Gross Margin Percentage (after adding the new labour cost)

Where:

- *Direct Labour Expense* = the additional cost you want to cover (e.g., new tradesperson, chef, production staff)
- *Gross Margin Percentage* = (Sales – COGS) ÷ Sales, expressed as a decimal, and updated to include the new direct labour in COGS

Example:

- Current gross margin = 50% (0.5 as a decimal)
- New direct labour cost = $60,000/year
- Updated gross margin after adding new labour = 45% (0.45)

Calculation:

- Required additional revenue = 60,000 ÷ 0.45 = $133,333

You'd need **$133,333 in extra sales** at the *new* gross margin to fully pay for that extra direct labour cost.

The sales you need to hire your new admin rockstar (indirect labour)

To work out how much *additional* revenue you need to generate to cover an overhead expense, you use this formula:

Required Additional Revenue
= Overhead Expense ÷ Gross margin

Where:

- *Overhead Expense* = the fixed cost you're trying to cover (e.g., new office rent, extra salary, software subscription)
- *Gross margin* = (Sales – COGS) ÷ Sales, expressed as a decimal

Example:

- Overhead expense = $60,000 per year
- Gross margin = 50% (0.5 as a decimal)

Calculation:

- Required additional revenue = 60,000 ÷ 0.5 = 120,000

So, you'd need $120,000 in additional sales at your current gross margin to cover that $60,000 expense.[4]

That's where it gets powerful for cashflow planning.

For overhead, your gross margin stays the same. For direct labour, the margin percentage drops, so you must calculate using the *reduced* percentage, otherwise you'll underestimate the sales you need.

George's rule

When your team says, "We need to hire," ask: *Is the hire direct or indirect?* Then calculate the margin and cashflow impact.

[4] This method is appropriate as long as there is capacity in COGS to deal with this additional revenue. If there is insufficient capacity in COGS, you need to recalculate margin percentage to allow for additional resource cost.

Cash timing and payroll: Avoiding the cycle mismatch

Never set a payroll cycle shorter than your cash collection cycle.

If you pay fortnightly but customers pay in 60 days, you've got a problem. Cash out is faster than cash in, so you can be profitable on paper yet run out of cash. Table 4 demonstrates how this can be done, with fortnightly wages of $10,000 and sales of $15,000. In the table you'll see the difference trading terms makes to your bank balance.

Sixty-day payment terms create a cash hole, while 14-day terms keep you cash positive from day one. It's a clear reminder that aligning or at least narrowing the gap between payroll and cash collection is critical to staying in control of your cashflow.

Fortnight	Wages paid	60 Days		14 Days	
		Money Received in 60 days	Cash position	Money Received in 14 days	Cash position
1	$10,000	$0	-$10,000	$15,000	$5,000
2	$10,000	$0	-$20,000	$15,000	$10,000
3	$10,000	$15,000	-$15,000	$15,000	$15,000

Table 4: Cash position with different payment terms

With 60-day terms, you're still $15,000 in the red by fortnight 3. With 14-day terms, you're cash positive from the very first fortnight. There is no cashflow gap. This is where we need to be so that we can be a business that is cashflow positive.

Solutions:

- Shorten customer payment terms
- Incentivise early payment
- Use direct debit
- Match inflows with outflows

This is one of the simplest, most powerful cashflow hacks you can implement.

Final word: Make hiring count

Hiring is a cashflow move, not just a people one.

It's easy to feel like a rockstar when your team grows. New hires feel like momentum. But if that hire isn't aligned with margin and revenue, you're just inflating overheads and shrinking your runway.

Smart founders don't just ask, "Can I afford the salary?" They consider, "Can I afford the impact on cashflow if this hire takes six months to deliver?"

So, before you make that next hire, ask:

- Will this person generate more profit margin than they cost?
- Will this person generate more cash for the business than it will take to pay them?
- Do my payment terms support this hire?
- Have I planned to avoid the Valley of Death (more about this in Day 17)?
- Will this role drive sustainable, compounding cashflow?

Hiring done well builds teams that grow the bank balance, not drain it.

Nail this, and you won't just grow your team. You'll grow a business that funds itself, scales without bleeding, and generates kickass cashflow.

Kickass Cashflow Power Move #5

Before hiring anyone, calculate how much more in sales you need to win so that you can pay them and retain your profitability. Because no profit means no cash.

"Assumptions are made, and most assumptions are wrong."

— Attributed to Albert Einstein

DAY 6

Mind the Gap: Margin vs. Markup

The dangerous assumptions that nearly sank a 40-year business

Not long ago, a successful manufacturing business that had been operating for more than four decades called us in to work with its team. They manufactured, assembled, and installed specialised equipment in local council parks and had a legacy of strong leadership, profitability, and steady growth. The founder had built it from scratch, providing not only for his own family but for his children and their families, too. Solid cash reserves. Smart investments. A real success story.

But things had started to change.

The founder had stepped back, and his three adult children stepped in: one to lead manufacturing, one to head up sales, and one as CEO. On the surface, everything looked fine. They were still getting monthly reports from their accountant. Sales were ticking along. People were busy.

But behind the scenes? Profitability was sinking. Cash reserves were draining. The only advice they heard from their accountant, month after month, was: "Profit is down, cash is getting tighter, you have to cut more costs." So they did. Again and again.

Still, the profit and cash kept sinking.

Three years in, with cash reserves drying up and family tensions rising, the CEO brought us in. They didn't know what was going wrong. The volume of work was still flowing, the team was busier than ever, but the cashflow didn't reflect that. That's when we delivered one of our signature Kickass Cashflow workshops and helped them build a One-Page Strategic Plan, a tool from the Scaling Up platform.

What happened next cracked the whole thing open.

The moment it clicked

In one of the training sessions with the sales support team, someone raised their hand and asked:

"Isn't markup the same as margin?"

It was the kind of question that made us stand still.

Why? Because it came from the person responsible for updating the price list every time a supplier raised their rates.

That single sentence explained everything. The pricing engine of the business had a fundamental misunderstanding at its core. No one had caught it. Each sibling had assumed the other was handling pricing correctly because that's what Dad had always done. They had abdicated the updating of the pricing list to the supply chain officer, who had no training or understanding of this fundamental difference.

To add to the complexity, the supply chain officer was a brilliant engineer, but English was his second language, and the two terms sounded interchangeable to him. It wasn't his fault. No one had checked his work, and no one had trained him properly. The siblings all assumed it was handled by the other... and guess what? The finger pointing started, and conversations became quite heated because that one question, that one moment, uncovered *millions of dollars in unrecoverable profit* and lost cash.

Here's the thing no one wants to admit in a boardroom: The biggest threats to your business aren't always external. They're inside the walls.

They're hidden in what you *assume* everyone knows. And they grow in the gaps between what gets said and what gets understood.

You don't lose millions overnight. You lose them slowly, quietly, through breakdowns in communication, roles that aren't clearly defined, and teams that are too proud to admit they don't understand the numbers.

Let this be your wake-up call: If your team can't confidently explain the difference between *markup* and *margin*, your cashflow is already bleeding. You just haven't seen the full damage yet.

Margin vs. markup: It's not just semantics

Let's break it down so this never happens to your business. This mistake happens more than you'd think, and it always costs you real money.

- *Margin* is how much gross margin you make on a sale, expressed as a percentage of the final selling price.
- *Markup* is how much you add to your costs to get to that selling price.

If your product costs $10 and you want a *50% margin*, you sell it for $20.

But if someone mistakenly applies a *50% markup*, they price it at $15.

That's a $5 mistake on every single sale.

Multiply that across 10,000 units? That's *$50,000 that's vanished out of your pocket.*

That's money you needed to pay your team, cover supplier bills, or reinvest in growth. And yet, most businesses don't catch it until the cashflow crisis is already happening.

The kicker? It could have been avoided with a single conversation. One check-in. One shared language. One moment of clarity.

Three game-changing lessons

- **Educate your whole team:** Don't silo financial understanding to the finance team. Your sales, ops, and pricing people need to understand margin and markup. This is the language of cashflow.
- **Pay attention to your "oxygen":** When cash gets tight, leaders stop listening. Literally. The brain goes into fight-or-flight. If someone had been truly listening when the "markup = margin" question was raised, the business could have saved years of pain.
- **Appoint a "Cashinator":** Someone must be accountable for approving pricing, reviewing margin, and enforcing trading terms. In the world of *Kickass Cashflow*, we call this person the Cashinator. Without clear ownership, you're flying blind and *hoping* someone is taking care of it, which usually means no one is. We'll cover this in depth on Day 24.

Why understanding Gross Margin Dollars matters for cashflow

If your Gross Margin Dollars are weak, your cashflow will never be right.

Period.

Gross Margin Dollars is the first signal that your pricing, cost structure, and customer alignment are working. It is the lever that fuels reinvestment, cushions downturns, and gives you control over your financial future. And it all starts with *everyone speaking the same financial language.*

And that's the first building block that builds unstoppable, cashflow-positive businesses, not assumptions that someone else has got it covered, not guesses, not fancy financial jargon, and not lost-in-translation mistakes.

If you think the problem is out there and doesn't apply to you or your team… think again.

In my experience, everyone politely nods that they understand, but when we bring out the calculators, the maths goes south, bleeding cash everywhere. Teach the language of margin and markup. And give your business the clarity it needs to grow stronger, smarter, and far more profitable, one well-priced, cash-generating sale at a time.

Kickass Cashflow Power Move #6

Cross-check pricing list calculations and changes every single time there's an update to your COGS.

Insist on educating yourself and your team about the difference between margin and markup. It's one of the simplest lessons that can save your business from cash burn.

DAY 7

It's Time to Slice and Dice Your Numbers

Good data early is better than perfect data too late.

Years ago, we built a simple table to visualise one of our clients' profitability and, wow, was it an eye-opener. On paper, their profit and loss statement told us they were making a total of $500,000 in Gross Margin Dollars. But when we sliced and diced the numbers by customer profitability, the story changed completely.

The table made it glaringly obvious: Their star performer (hello, Customer #1!) was delivering big returns and joy to the team, while others, yes, we mean Customer #8, were quietly draining time, energy, and profit. Years later, we discovered waterfall graphs, in Verne Harnish's groundbreaking book *Scaling Up: How a Few Companies Make it... and Why the Rest Don't*. These graphs tell the story with clarity and speed that no spreadsheet can match.

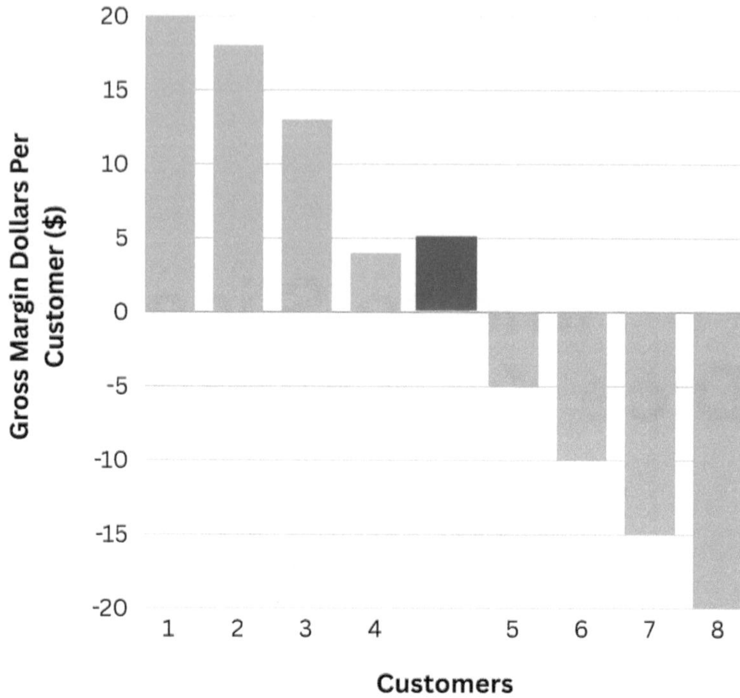

Figure 5: Waterfall graph

Even though Customer #8 brought in almost the same revenue as their top customer, the Gross Margin Dollars couldn't have been more different. Customer #1 was a dream: profitable, respectful, paid on time every single time, and easy to work with.

But Customer #8? Their demands, inefficiencies, and poor behaviour were dragging down our client's team and Gross Margin Dollars because they cost so much more time to serve.

So, on the surface, when we averaged out their Gross Margin Dollars, things looked okay, but when we sliced and diced the numbers by customer Gross Margin Dollars, it was crystal clear that #8 was draining them, and if all their clients were like #8, they would have quickly gone under.

The graph lifted the lid on the business's performance, and it was the kind of truth that once you see it, you can't unsee it!

That's when it hit me: Their best customer was subsidising the bad behaviour of their worst performing customer. In fact, we had to dig deeper into customers #5 to #8 and see what was going on. To start with though, we went into bat and dealt with #8, "spring cleaning" them off their client list.

We gently suggested that it might be time for Customer #8 to move on, but, of course, he didn't want to leave. So, our client acted: they doubled his price and set very clear boundaries around how his company needed to treat their team.

To our surprise, Customer #8 started toeing the line and treating our client's team with respect, but eventually the bad behaviour and sloppiness returned, so they graciously let him go.

This bold move paid off, and they repeated it with other, similar clients.

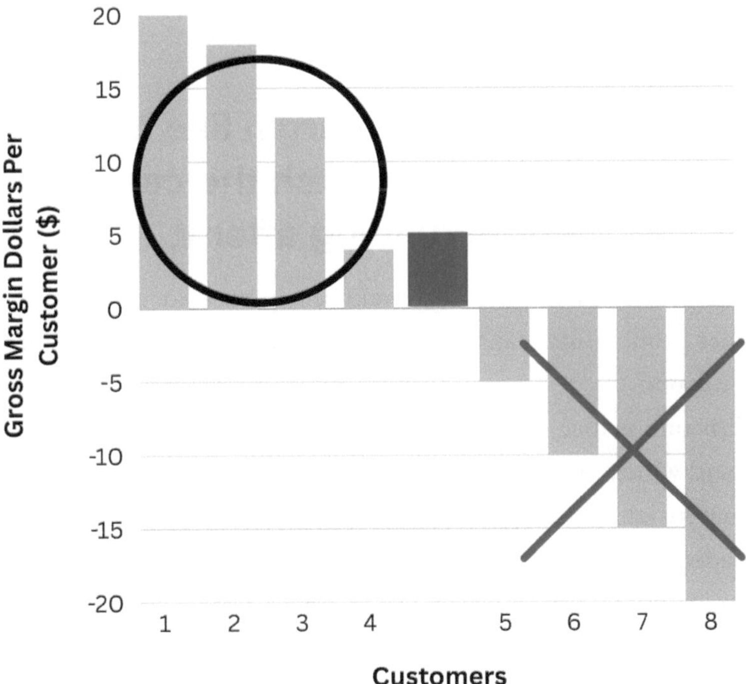

Figure 6: Focusing on the right customers

Once our client made the shift, they saw a real impact. They restructured the business to eliminate noise and confidently said goodbye to loss-making clients and team members who no longer fit.

By letting go of clients who weren't a fit, either financially or culturally, our client freed up space, energy, and resources to serve the right customers even better. The business became significantly healthier. They were doing the same amount of work, but with better Gross Margin Dollars and a whole lot less stress and eventually loads of cash in the bank.

The amazing thing? By simply letting go of their loss-making customers, their Gross Margin Dollars more than tripled from $500,000 to $1.7 million in just one year. And here's the kicker: They did it by doing less work! That's the power of focusing on the right customers. Crazy cool, right?

The team and the owners were happier, and yes, they wish they had done it years ago.

Guard your gross margin like it's the crown jewels and watch the cashflow come running after it

As a business owner, you also want the power to create your own customer profitability – and that's where a waterfall graph becomes your secret weapon.

With one glance, you can see exactly which customers drive your profit and which ones quietly drain it dry. Sure, you could try to deliver the same insight with a spreadsheet, but in my experience, spreadsheets overloaded with numbers do one thing: paralyse a team. Too much data and suddenly no one wants to make a decision because it all feels too hard.

A waterfall graph cuts through that noise. It makes the truth obvious – instantly. You'll know which customers are a joy to work with and which ones need a hard decision. Visuals get everyone on the same page fast, aligned on what action to take, and ready to move.

Your accountant might hand you a tidy set of numbers, but if they're all mashed together, the magic is gone. You can't spot the patterns, the leaks, or the gold mines hiding in plain sight. And life's too short to let a bully customer with "great revenue" hold your business hostage. Don't get hoodwinked. Do the analysis, trust what you find, and back yourself to make it right.

If you're struggling to take control of your cashflow, fighting to get your head above water, and can't see the forest for the trees, the problem isn't you. The problem is how financial information is being presented to you. Numbers don't have to be complicated; they just have to be shown in a way that makes decisions crystal clear. And for me? Waterfall graphs are one of my all-time favourite tools to make that happen.

Because once you can see your business clearly, you'll never let the wrong customer steal your profit, or your peace of mind, again.

When Mac Powolny, CEO, began working with Performance 7, his company, Nautitech, wanted to scale up more rapidly. The 25-year-old firm, based in New South Wales, Australia, develops innovative, patented products for the mining industry – which allows it to avoid competing on price. An internal "Innovation Council" vets new product ideas at the company, which is even more focused on successful product launches than new product development. Thanks to this approach, the company has maintained strong Gross Margin Dollars and has encouraged the sales team to focus on margin targets, not just revenue. The company has also strengthened its supply chain to stay resilient during disruptions.

A data-driven approach, coupled with the Performance 7 tools, has allowed the company to accelerate growth and scale rapidly, expanding in 8 years from 35 employees to nearly 60 today. The company closely tracks Gross Margin Dollars in its detailed financial reporting, which includes budgets, actuals, and variance analyses by product group and geographic markets. For instance, one set of data looks at their products, which are intrinsically safe lights and cameras. "You can immediately see how you perform," says Powolny.

While sales grew 12% last year, the metric that really mattered was the increase in Gross Margin Dollars, and that jumped up by a healthy 21%.

Why regularly reviewing job profitability makes sense

Taking the time to review job or client profitability, ideally as often as possible, can pay off in a big way, even if the process feels a bit messy. For starters, it helps you nail your cost estimates and stay in control of spending. No more guesswork when it's time to quote the next job! With better insights into your true costs, you can set prices that are competitive *and* profitable. That means stronger Gross Margin Dollars and healthier cashflow.

But the benefits don't stop there. Job costing also helps you manage your resources more effectively. When you know exactly where your labour and materials are going, you can make smarter decisions that lead to better results and a more financially sound business.

Build momentum, not complexity

In my early days, the most successful clients weren't obsessing over spreadsheets; they were making quick, confident decisions. They trusted their instincts, used rough estimates wisely, and course corrected as needed. As your business grows and things get more complex, there'll be time to level up your tools, and maybe even to make job profitability a monthly focus. But right now? If your cashflow is under stress, then taking action beats waiting for software perfection. Don't wait for the bookkeeper or accountant to solve it for you, it's way simpler than that: pen, paper, and a handful of invoices and bills will help get to the bottom of what's going on within hours, not days or weeks. Start simple, stay focused, and protect your cash.

Forget perfect: Aim for progress

The best estimators aren't waiting around for the ideal software or complicated systems. Some of the sharpest business minds I've worked with could work out rough numbers on the back of an envelope faster than I could open my calculator app!

Dump non-profitable product or service lines

It's also essential to identify and eliminate non-profitable product or service lines. These are what we refer to as CRaP: "Can't Realise any Profit." CRaP products and services or customers are those that cost more to serve than they bring in revenue.

Not all customers or products and services contribute equally to your bottom line. High-maintenance customers or low-margin products and services can quickly drain resources, reducing profitability. By identifying these CRaP areas, you can focus on the products and services and customers that drive real growth and profitability. Strategies for dealing with CRaP include focusing on profitable products and services, optimising marketing efforts towards high-value customers and improving customer service efficiency.

Waterfall graphs are a very powerful way to explain the numbers to a leadership team making decisions. What the accountants tell us: "You made $150,000 Gross Margin Dollars. Congratulations. The industry average is $95,000 – well done." Here is what I'd like you to ask: "Can you please slice and dice the numbers so that they tell us a better story? Which customers generated the margin, and which ones drained it?"

To which they will take a sample set and show you something like the graph in Figure 6.

The hidden power of focusing on customer margin dollars (and why our client eventually said goodbye to Customer #8)

The result? More profit, less stress.

BUSINESS OWNER'S TIP:
Your path to peace: The waterfall graph
Slice and dice your Gross Margin Dollars and create a waterfall graph. These graphs easily explain which clients are profitable and which ones need adjusting. As a business owner, you probably have a gut feeling about how the numbers are working out and which clients are better to work with than others. However, creating a graph like this makes it very clear which clients deserve to be spoiled and have all your attention and which customers you need to rethink.

I recommend you create these waterfall graphs per product, per location, per salesperson. The list is endless. Graphs get your point across faster and easier than any spreadsheet packed with data. Never underestimate the power of a beautifully crafted graph to drive kickass cashflow decisions. Use it and make it one of your superpowers.

Why you should lose your loss leaders

While we're on this topic, let's clear up one of the biggest myths in business: that loss leaders are a smart strategy. They're not. Unless you're a giant retailer with deep pockets, advanced analytics, and a rock-solid plan to upsell at scale, then selling a product at a loss just to "get people in the door" can drain your Gross Margin Dollars faster than you can say, "cashflow crisis."

Too many businesses adopt this tactic without fully understanding the maths and then wonder why they're running at full speed and still bleeding cash. A loss leader without a clear path to profitable follow-up sales isn't a strategy; it's sabotage. If your business model relies on giving value away and hoping it'll convert later, take a step back. You're not just losing margin; you're setting your business up on a very slippery slope to destruction. No Gross Margin Dollars, no profit, no cash.

The takeaway

To start making great cashflow decisions, you need to rely on great reports. As a leader, it's okay for you to push back on the accounting reports and start asking probing questions about the true source of your Gross Margin Dollars and cashflow.

As we discussed, not all sales are created equal. And not every customer deserves a place in your business. When you take a closer look at your numbers, you might be surprised who's fuelling your cashflow and who's insidiously draining it. By uncovering *where your high-gross margin work lives*, you put yourself in a position to make smarter, faster decisions.

And when you regularly clean house by tightening your client list, backing your team, and letting go of what no longer serves your goals, you won't just be protecting your profit – *you'll unlock cashflow momentum.*

Go and create those waterfall graphs and power your business to run leaner, lighter, and generate stronger, more reliable cashflow. This is how you scale with confidence. This is how you put yourself on a winning cashflow path.

Kickass Cashflow Power Move #7

Unlock your slicing and dicing superpower by creating a waterfall graph to determine which customers are your most valuable.

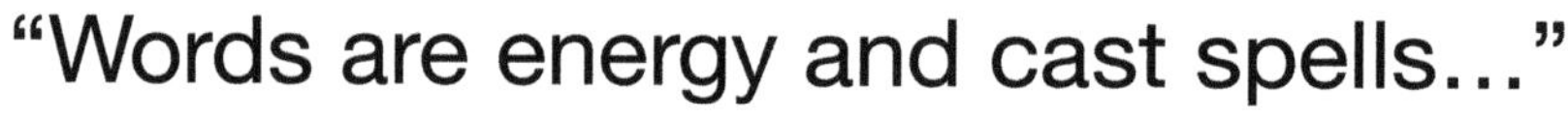

“Words are energy and cast spells…”

— Attributed to Bruce Lee

DAY 8

Language Matters: Talk $, Not %

I was invited to observe an executive team's monthly meeting in my coaching practice. The company designed and installed specialised farming equipment. Its turnover was $10m, but it had made no profit in the last few years.

The CEO had been in his seat for the past two years and had hired highly qualified and experienced executives from big corporations. They were on big pay packets. The CEO hoped that the executives could help him implement new ideas to resuscitate the business.

During the meeting, one exec shared how his team had recently sold some items at 55% gross margin, and high-fives were shared all around the room. I let the conversation continue as he took centre stage.

After this conversation soaked up 15 minutes (one-quarter of our allocated time for the meeting), I had to ask, "How much was that in Gross Margin Dollars?" He replied, $325. The oxygen quickly left the room… We couldn't even pay the staff amenities bill that month with the $325. The meeting moved on.

It's important to *emphasise* the importance of talking about margin *dollars* and not percentages. Effective communication between you and your team in this area of your business is one of the greatest productivity hacks you will ever implement in your business.

I'm a true believer that *the more frequently teams talk to each other, the faster we scale.* Having a common language with your team during these conversations supports one of your most valuable and expensive business resources – your people – in collaborating more easily and accelerates decision-making.

When teams communicate effectively, everyone gets onto the same page faster and speaks the same language. This clarity reduces rework and eliminates ambiguity in decision-making, helping your people operate at peak efficiency. As a result, your cashflow improves, as your entire team stays aligned and empowered to move forward together.

Ditch the jargon and talk real dollars

When a small- to medium-sized business starts to grow, it's easy to focus on speaking gross margin percentage. This would be fine if you were a massive multinational company with hundreds of millions in turnover, but for medium-sized businesses with tight profitability and cashflow, it is critical to prioritise the right work. In short, *we don't eat percentages; we eat dollars.* We pay people's salaries in dollars. You take home at the end of the day dollars, not percentages. Focus on Gross Margin *Dollars*, and you won't have to worry about making payroll.

I've lost count of how many times I've asked a business owner, "How's your gross margin looking?" and been told, "Oh, about 35%." Then I'll pause, look them in the eye, and say, "Okay, but how many dollars is that?" Most of the time, the answer is silence. Gross margin percentage has become a comfort metric for many owners. It's easy to remember and it looks nice on a report. But percentages don't pay your rent, your wages, your tax bill, or your suppliers. Only Gross Margin Dollars do.

Imagine two products:

- Product A has a 50% gross margin on $10,000 in sales – that's $5,000 in gross margin.
- Product B has a 30% gross margin on $100,000 in sales – that's $30,000 in gross margin.

If you only looked at percentages, you'd think Product A is the "better" product. But in reality, Product B generates six times the Gross Margin Dollars. And those dollars are what keep the lights on.

This is why I tell every business owner I coach: **You can't spend a percentage**. You can't walk into the bank with a gross margin percentage and pay down your loan. You can't hand your landlord a 42% gross margin and expect the rent to be covered. Dollars are the fuel your business runs on. Percentages just tell you how efficiently you're generating that fuel.

Does that mean percentages are useless? Absolutely not. Gross margin percentage is a powerful indicator of pricing strength, cost control, and efficiency. But it's only half the picture. The full picture comes when you pair the percentage with the dollar value – because that tells you both how well you're performing and how much you've actually got to work with.

Now, here's where many businesses fall short: They look at percentages in the boardroom, but they never translate it into plain English for the team. Your team might hear "our margin is 40%" and think everything's fine. But if that 40% only equates to $200,000 in gross margin this month, and your fixed costs are $450,000, you're in trouble. And they need to know that.

This is why I push my clients to present gross margin in dollars first, percentage second, when talking to their teams. It's about connecting the numbers to reality. Tell them, "We brought in $85,000 in gross margin this month. Our overhead is $60,000, so we have $25,000 left before tax." That's a message that lands. People understand dollars in a way they don't understand percentages.

I once worked with a manufacturing business that was obsessed with keeping their gross margin percentage above 45%. They were so focused on the percentage that they passed up on several large-volume orders with slightly lower percentage margins. When we ran the numbers, those "lower margins in percentage" orders would have delivered an extra $780,000 in Gross Margin Dollars, enough to cover two new hires and upgrade their equipment. They had been so busy protecting the percentage that they forgot the goal was to grow the dollars.

On the flip side, I've seen businesses chase sales at the expense of both gross margin percentage and dollars. They'll take on big contracts with razor-thin margins, thinking "we'll make it up in volume." That's a dangerous game. If the margin dollars aren't there to cover your fixed costs and generate a profit, you're just working harder to stand still – or worse, to go backwards.

The sweet spot is understanding both: Use gross margin percentage to check the health of your pricing and cost control but always track and target Gross Margin Dollars to make sure you have the cash to pay the bills and grow the business.

Communicating this to your team is just as important as understanding it yourself. Imagine your sales team knows that every extra $10,000 in Gross Margin Dollars moves the business closer to funding their next pay rise or securing the resources they've been asking for. Suddenly, they're not just chasing sales, they're focused on chasing *profitable* sales. When everyone in the business starts thinking in Gross Margin Dollars, decision-making changes.

You start asking better questions:

- "If we discount, how much Gross Margin Dollars will we lose?"
- "If we invest in this marketing campaign, how much Gross Margin Dollars will it generate?"
- "If we shift our sales mix, how will it affect our Gross Margin Dollars?"

Percentages can hide the truth. Dollars tell the truth.

And in business, the truth is you don't bank percentages, you bank dollars.

So, next time you review your financials, flip the order. Lead first by asking: How many Gross Margin Dollars did we make? Then: What percentage is that? Lead your conversations, your planning, and your team meetings with the dollars – because they're the only thing you can actually spend.

This is the most important power move you can make in your conversations if you're running a small- or medium-sized business. Percentages can muddy the waters. They sound smart, but they don't always drive smart decisions. Talking in Gross Margin *Dollars* gets your whole team on the same page, fast. It cuts through confusion, removes the guesswork, and gives everyone from marketing to ops to sales a clear, practical way to make better calls in the moment.

Leadership teams don't need more complexity. They need clarity. And when your entire leadership team is speaking a common, cash-focused language, meetings get sharper, decisions get stronger, and momentum builds faster.

So, stop pretending, start simplifying, and get your team fluent in the one language that truly grows a business's *cashflow clarity*.

Kickass Cashflow Power Move #8

Talk dollars, not percentages – you'll work together as a team faster.

“We loved with a love that was more than love. But sometimes, love, however deep, is not enough when timing is off.”

— Inspired by Edgar Allan Poe

DAY 9

Don't Let Trading Terms Kill Your Cashflow

Lochie had a great business. He made premium, all-natural dog biscuits that were handcrafted, beautifully packaged, and beloved by pet owners. As demand grew, he started selling through distributors.

He struck two deals at once. Both looked great on the surface. Both promised strong volumes. But what happened next would become a textbook case in how trading terms can make or break your business cashflow. Lochie, a small business owner with a great product and a solid vision, initially had no idea how much damage slow-paying customers could do.

Let's look at two scenarios that highlight the hidden impact of trading terms on cashflow. In the first, customers pay on delivery, meaning cash hits your account immediately. In the second, customers are given extended payment terms, and the wait for that cash begins. Same sales, same margins, but the timing of when you get paid can be the difference between strong, predictable cashflow and a constant scramble to cover expenses.

Scenario 1: The dream distributor (cash on delivery)

Distributor A was a small operation. They promised $100k orders per month. They ordered modest quantities, but they *paid Cash on Delivery (COD).* Lochie dropped off the biscuits, and money hit his account the same day. No delays. No chasing.

This gave Lochie instant liquidity. He had cash in hand to

- pay for ingredients,
- cover wages,
- fund marketing, and
- reinvent and restock.

Every sale felt like forward momentum. The cycle was clean, simple, and sustainable.

Scenario 2: The delay distributor (with long payment terms)

Distributor B was a bigger name. Larger footprint, more customers. Their first order was huge at $800k, with a promise for $150k per month orders. Lochie was thrilled. The only catch? 30-day, end-of-month (EOM) payment terms.

That meant if he invoiced them on March 2, they'd pay by April 30. And that's *if* they paid on time. They didn't.

Every invoice dragged out *another 30 days.* Suddenly, Lochie was waiting 90 days or more to see any money. Meanwhile, he had to front the cost of production; pay for packaging, shipping, and labour; and fund restocking for the next batch.

He had all the paperwork showing strong sales but zero cash in the bank to keep the business moving.

Guess what he started doing?

He increased his overdraft limit.

He stopped paying himself.

He delayed paying suppliers.

And eventually, he considered turning away new orders because he couldn't afford to fulfil them.

Lochie's two distributors taught him a painful but essential truth: Big margin dollars are not enough. You need trading terms that work for you, not against you, terms that accelerate cash in and delay cash out.

Distributor B may have offered bigger orders and higher profile customers, but the delayed cash created a bottleneck. The more he sold, the worse his cashflow got.

Sound familiar?

Lochie learned something every founder, CEO, and business owner eventually learns the hard way: You can be profitable on paper and still broke at the bank. Why? Because cash doesn't move when you send an invoice; that happens when you get paid.

It doesn't matter how great your product is. It doesn't matter how much you sell. If you don't have control over your *trading terms*, your cashflow will suffer, and so will your business.

Too many businesses fall into this trap. They chase big contracts without locking in the right payment terms and wonder why they're making sales but feel like they're suffocating financially.

Smart pricing + smart terms = kickass cashflow

You already know pricing is powerful. It fuels the margin and drives the cash that keeps your business alive. But *if your money is stuck in someone else's bank account*, what's the point?

The smartest businesses do both:

- *They price for margin*, so every sale delivers real cash.
- They set trading terms that protect their cashflow, so they're never left waiting and worrying about when the money will come in.

When pricing and payment terms work together, the business becomes unstoppable.

How Lochie turned the ship around

Lochie learned quickly. He renegotiated with Distributor B. He changed their terms from 30-day EOM to strict 14-day payment after delivery, with late fees built in. Distributor B pushed back. He held firm.

He also

- required deposits on large orders to cover ingredients,
- offered *small* discounts for early payments in full (tightly managed and aligned with his strategy),
- created clear consequences for late payers, and
- kept a tight eye on accounts receivable and flagged issues early.

And here's what happened:

His cashflow improved.

He stopped relying on overdrafts.

He paid himself again.

And he scaled confidently, without an uncomfortable hallway conversation with the bookkeeper that cash is tight again.

BUSINESS OWNER'S TIP:
Trading terms are negotiable

You don't have to accept whatever terms a customer puts in front of you. You can negotiate. You should negotiate. Your cashflow sanity depends on it.

Set terms that work for *your business,* not just theirs. Protect your working capital. And if someone doesn't respect your terms, they may not be the kind of partner you want long term.

A big sale that doesn't pay on time is more dangerous than a series of small ones that do. You can't pay your team with promises and "big-brand jobs". You can't pay rent with invoices being avoided in someone's inbox.

Build your muscle

Setting smart trading terms is a negotiation muscle you need to build, just like pricing. You develop it by setting clear policies, having the confidence to stand by them, and building a culture where *cashflow is queen.*

So, the next time you're about to say yes to a big deal, ask one question: **When will I get paid?**

Because if you can get your *pricing right* and your *payment terms tight*, you're building a business with strength, stability, and staying power. Businesses are valued more highly when they have strong, predictable cashflow, not just accounting profits. In fact, **buyers will pay a premium for a business with robust cashflow over one that is merely profitable on paper.**

And that's how you win.

For Lochie's business, the ultimate goal is to flatten the cashflow curve to get rid of the sharp peaks and troughs that cause stress and uncertainty. When cashflow is steady, Lochie isn't scrambling for funding in the bad months or letting idle cash sit around in the good months. Instead, he's in control, with the confidence to plan, invest, and grow.

Let's see it in action. Table 5 shows Lochie's business under poor trading terms that choke cashflow. Table 6 shows the same business with improved terms, transforming the cashflow curve from a rollercoaster into a smooth runway for sustainable growth.

Before Cashflow Planning

Week	1	2	3	4	5	6	7
Opening Cash Balance	0	-10,000	-13,500	-13,500	3,000	3,000	3,000
Supplier payment	-10,000						
wages paid		-3,500		-3,500			
customer pays 50%							
customer pays				20,000			20,000
Closing cash balance	-10,000	-13,500	-13,500	3,000	3,000	3,000	23,000

Table 5: Before: Poor trading terms hurt cashflow

Insight: Despite high revenue from a large distributor, Lochie operates in negative cash for weeks due to 30-day EOM terms, followed by delayed customer payments. Cashflow is under strain, even with strong sales.

After Cashflow Planning

Week	1	2	3	4	5	6	7
Opening Cash Balance	-	5,000	1,500	1,500	8,000	8,000	8,000
Supplier payment	- 10,000						
wages paid		- 3,500		- 3,500			
customer pays 50%							
customer pays	15,000			10,000			15,000
Closing cash balance	5,000	1,500	1,500	8,000	8,000	8,000	23,000

Table 6: After: Improved trading terms create positive cashflow

Insight: Lochie renegotiates payment terms, securing upfront deposits and shorter payment cycles. As a result, he maintains a healthy cash buffer from the start, avoids negative balances, and funds operations stress-free.

Figure 7 shows exactly what happened when Lochie took control of his trading terms: Same product. Same revenue. Different cash at bank outcome during the seven-week period.

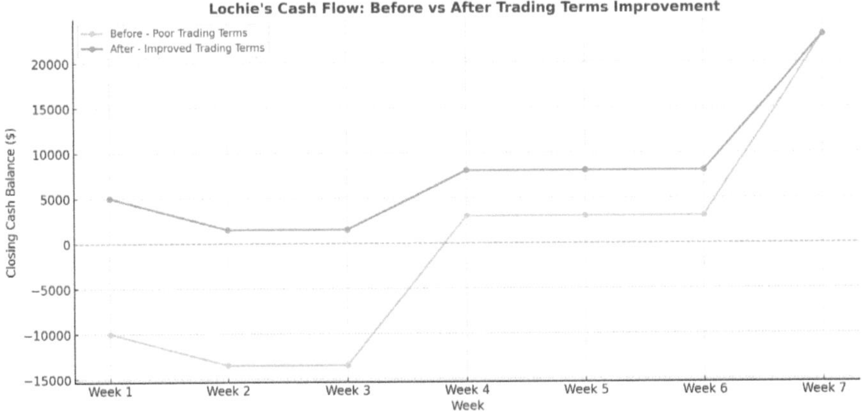

Figure 7: Before and after trading terms improvement

When he required upfront payments and locked in better terms, he stopped the cash bleed, got out of the red, and finally had breathing room.

The ultimate goal is to be cashflow positive throughout the delivery of any project. And if you can get paid in advance, before you even start a project, even better. Your head will be in the right place, and you will deliver an excellent service to that customer.

What is customer factoring?

One option for high-growth businesses under cashflow strain is customer factoring.

Customer factoring, also known as *invoice factoring*, is when you *sell your unpaid invoices* to a finance company (called a *factor*) to get cash now instead of waiting for your customer to pay.

Let's say you've invoiced a client for $50,000 on 30-day terms. You need the cash now to pay staff, buy supplies, or take on new work. So instead of waiting a month, you sell that invoice to a factoring company. They give you, say, *80-90% upfront*, and then pay the rest (minus their fees) when the customer pays.

How it works (simple example):

- You invoice your customer for $50,000.
- You send that invoice to a factoring company.
- They give you $45,000 now (90%).
- When the customer pays, the factor keeps a *fee* (usually 2-5%) and gives you the rest.
- You get your money *faster*, but you pay for the privilege.

Benefits of factoring

- **Faster cashflow:** No more waiting 30, 60, or 90 days. You get paid almost immediately, so you can keep moving.
- **It funds growth without debt:** It's not a loan, so you're not taking on extra debt or diluting equity. You're just unlocking money that's already yours.
- **Covers the "cash gap":** Bridges the period between when you do the work and when you get paid, making it especially helpful for payroll-heavy or project-based businesses.
- **Outsources collections:** Some factoring companies also handle chasing payments, saving your team time and awkward phone calls.

Costs and considerations

- **It's not free:** Typical fees range from *2% to 5%* of the invoice value and may be even more if the customer is high-risk or slow to pay. That eats into your margin.
- **Customer-experience risk:** Your customers might be contacted by the factoring company. If not managed well, that can impact relationships or raise questions.
- **You still own the risk (sometimes):** If the customer doesn't pay, *you* might be on the hook. This depends on whether you use *recourse factoring* (you're responsible) or *non-recourse* (they absorb the loss).
- **Short-term fix, not a long-term strategy:** Factoring helps you smooth over cash gaps, but if your Gross Margin Dollars are tight or your pricing's wrong, it won't solve the root cause.

So, should you factor?

Factoring is a *cashflow tool*, but it eats at your margin too, as you have to pay for the finance facility. If you have a healthy business with slow-paying customers and strong Gross Margin Dollars, it can be a smart way to keep moving without taking on debt.

If a customer refuses to budge on payment terms, factoring could be a solution, but only if you've built it into your pricing for that customer. For example, charging Distributor B a 5% premium covers the cashflow gap and protects your business. That's far better than bleeding out your Gross Margin Dollars.

And if you're always factoring just to stay afloat, it's a warning sign. Time to look at your pricing, costs, and payment terms.

Final word: Money isn't made until it's collected

This chapter isn't just about getting paid; it's about reclaiming control. Because when you set the terms, you set the tone for how your business runs. Profit means nothing if the money never lands. Sales don't matter if you can't meet payroll. You are not a bank for your customers. So, stop playing nice with payment terms that hurt your business. Start building the kind of muscle Lochie did. The kind that backs great products with powerful cashflow discipline. Because when the money moves on your terms, your business doesn't just survive, it thrives. And that's how real founders lead. With clarity. With strength. And with cold, hard cash in the bank.

Kickass Cashflow Power Move #9

Know the timing of your cash inflows and outflows.

"...positive cashflow got me through downturns and allowed us to beat the competition!"

— Andrew Banks, Co-founder Morgan & Banks, Founder Talent2 International, Shark on TV series *Shark Tank*

DAY 10

Fuel Before Flight: How Marginal Cashflow Powers Real Growth

Marginal cashflow: The real currency of scale

This is a good place to start bringing all the concepts shared in the previous chapters together and set the record straight, once and for all: Profit is not cash. It's not even close. You can post a six-figure profit on paper and still be haemorrhaging cash in real life. That disconnect is where a lot of businesses, especially fast-growing ones, find themselves in trouble.

And here's why: They don't understand marginal cashflow.

What is marginal cashflow?

Marginal cashflow is the real-world impact on your bank account when you make *one more sale*. On paper, it sounds straightforward: Sell something for $10, it costs you $6 to deliver, you've made a $4 gross margin. Easy win, right?

But reality doesn't run on paper. Let's say you pay your supplier in 2 weeks (14 days), but your customer takes 6 weeks (42 days) to pay you. You've now created a **cash gap**. That $6 COGS leaves your account before the $10 payment arrives. Until payment arrives, your bank balance is lower than it was before the sale.

That's negative marginal cashflow, when every extra sale burns through your cash instead of building it. And this is exactly how businesses can grow revenue and still run out of money. The bigger the gap between cash out and cash in, the more each extra sale quietly drains your bank account dry.

This is why we say you don't scale with profit.

You scale using cash. And it's by far my favourite way to scale. If you nail this, you have achieved pure market fit, and your customers are funding your growth. **The cheapest cash you will ever find to fund your growth is your customers' cash.**

If you don't know how much *actual* cash every new sale generates (or burns), then growth isn't your golden ticket. It may be a ticking time bomb.

The hidden drain of trading terms

As seen in the previous chapter, your trading terms (how long it takes to get paid vs. how quickly you pay others) can make or break your cashflow, regardless of how strong your Gross Margin Dollars is. Get the trading terms wrong, and even a profitable business can find itself starved of cash.

Let's define the two key trading term metrics you need to track:

- **Receivables days:** How long your customers take to pay you
- **Payables days:** How long you have to pay your suppliers

When your marginal cashflow is negative, you're stuck finding money to plug the gap until customers finally pay up. That might mean raiding your personal savings, leaning on an overdraft, taking out a short-term loan, or pushing back payments to suppliers, all of which cost you money or strain valuable relationships.

If you don't take action by getting in control of your trading terms, speeding up collections, or managing inventory smarter, then you end up on a hamster wheel, constantly funding the gap instead of filling your bank account. The longer you ignore it, the bigger and uglier that cash hole gets. This isn't just a little financial leak, it's a full-blown drain on your energy, focus, and freedom.

Use the marginal cashflow lens to make smart moves

This is the tool that flips the game: Knowing your *marginal cashflow per sale* puts you back in the driver's seat.

With this lens, you'll know

- whether every new sale grows or drains your cash,
- if your trading terms are setting you up for scale or strangling your bank account,
- where to negotiate smarter terms with suppliers or customers, and
- when to pause, tighten, or throttle your growth to protect your cash runway.

The Kickass Cashflow Checklist: Are you scaling smart?

Here's your marginal cashflow reality check. Ask yourself:

- Is my Gross Margin Dollars consistent and high enough to generate surplus cash?
- Do I know how many days it takes to get paid by my customers (receivables days)?
- Do I know how quickly I must pay my suppliers (payables days)?
- Do I have to outlay cash for stock, wages, or delivery before I get paid?
- Does each additional sale put cash *into* or take cash *out* of my bank account?
- Have I modelled different growth scenarios using cash, not just P&L projections?

If you answered "no" to more than two of those questions, *stop*.

Don't add another product, hire another person, or chase another client until you've figured out your marginal cashflow.

Marginal Cashflow Worksheet

To help you calculate this, use the **Marginal Cashflow Worksheet**. It breaks down the components of your cashflow:

- Unit economics
  - Selling price per unit
  - Direct cost per unit (COGS)
  - Gross margin per unit (selling price – COGS)
- Trading terms impact
  - Days to receive payment
  - Days to pay suppliers

  - Inventory holding days (if applicable)
  - Net cashflow gap (how long you're out of pocket)
- Working capital impact
  - Cash required upfront for each sale
  - Timing of outflows vs inflows
  - Cash generated (or burnt) per unit of growth

Marginal cashflow by product: Profitability vs. Cash Impact

At Performance 7, we've developed a ranking tool as part of our coaching journey, and we run every client through it. It's designed to give business owners a clear, side-by-side view of each product's profitability and its real cashflow impact. By combining Gross Margin Dollars and percentages with trading terms (receivables and payables days), this tool quickly reveals which products generate cash and which quietly drain it.

A product with a high gross margin but slow customer payment can be more damaging to your cash position than a lower-margin product with fast payment terms. We use this table to help clients decide which products to prioritise, which terms to renegotiate, and where pricing or operational changes are needed to protect and improve liquidity.

By plugging your numbers into this worksheet, you'll see in real terms whether you're scaling a cash-positive business or digging a deeper hole.

Use it monthly. Put it to work for you when planning growth. Break it out every time a supplier changes their price or their terms on your invoices. Reference it every time before you take on a big customer or new supplier. Use it before you raise prices or sign new contracts. This is your secret kickass weapon.

For a downloadable worksheet go to:

www.KickassCashflow.com

Kickass moves you can make with this insight

Once you've nailed your marginal cashflow, you can start playing offence:

- **Negotiate better payment terms:** Get paid faster or extend supplier terms to shorten the cash gap.
- **Tighten inventory cycles:** Don't sit on stock. Sell it fast. Improve inventory turnover.
- **Raise prices strategically:** Even a 5% lift in price can radically improve your cash buffer.
- **Slow down if you must:** Scaling too fast without cash is reckless. Dial back to stay alive.
- **Build a buffer:** Forecast your cash needs 90 days ahead. Stay ahead of the wave.

Final word: You're not here to look good on paper

You're not building a business to impress an accountant or win a trophy for highest sales turnover ever. You're endeavouring to build something real, something that feeds your family and funds your future, an asset you could one day sell – one that gives you the freedom to say yes or no on *your* terms.

And that doesn't happen with profit trapped on paper. Success happens with cash in the bank, accessible, predictable, and powerful.

So, here's the formula to remember:

Great margin dollars + strong trading terms = kickass cashflow

The most valuable companies don't scale with theoretical profit. They multiply their valuation by building a business that is a cashflow-positive money-making machine.

They scale with cash.

That's how you stop spinning your wheels. That's how you lead with confidence. And that's how you build a business that doesn't just grow, it lasts.

Remember to ask "how much cash is this new sale generating or consuming?"

Kickass Cashflow Power Move #10

Calculate your marginal cashflow per product and or service line.

SECTION 2

Know the Math or Feel the Burn LTVC > CAC[5]

No More Spray and Pray: How Marketing Attracts Leads That Pay and Stay

Which Hat is Your Sales Team Wearing?

Sales Teams Pay Attention: Cashflow is All in *Your* Timing

Shaken, Not Stirred: Your Cashflow Cocktail

Know the Real Cost of Acquiring a Customer

Lifetime Value of a Customer

---

5 LTVC = Lifetime Value of a Customer = Margin Dollars generated by a customer
CAC = Customer Acquisition Costs

Hang in there…

Recently, I fielded this text from a private equity investor: *I need to work out how much to invest in marketing.*

My response: *If the maths makes sense, keep pumping in the cash.*

In this section, I'm going to share with you a calculation that very few get their head around. This is where spray and pray, and spinning wheels, get held to account. This is where the maths does make sense and hyper cash happens.

“Obsess over customers, not competitors.”

— Jeff Bezos

DAY 11

No More Spray and Pray: How Marketing Attracts Leads That Pay and Stay

Okay, get ready, I'm about to ruffle some feathers. This is where I see businesses burn the most cash. Like, take-a-blowtorch-to-a-pallet-of-money kind of burn.

Marketing is often treated like a magic wand. Hire a flashy agency, throw cash at social media, build a sleek website, and boom, the customers will just roll in, right?

Wrong.

The real world doesn't get results like that. And deep down, you know it.

If you're serious about building a business with strong, sustainable cashflow, it's time to take a hard look at your marketing strategy and where it's being driven from.

Brutal Fact: Marketing strategy belongs to your board, the owners, the directors, and the leadership team, not to a digital agency scraping Google, TikTok, and Instagram for trends.

And when that responsibility gets handed off? You lose control of your cash because the marketing agency doesn't understand your business's marginal cashflow per product that they are promoting.

Why marketing isn't a guessing game

Marketing isn't about going viral. It's about generating qualified leads, the ones that convert, pay on time, and come back for more. That kind of marketing is strategic. Targeted. Data-driven. And once you've mastered marginal cashflow, you're ready to go to the next level of growth.

Marketing's primary objective is to generate marketing qualified leads. These are prospects who fit your ideal customer profile, have engaged with your brand, and are ready for your sales team to close.

And yet, what I see time and time again is this:

Founders and CEOs are abdicating strategy to an outsourced team with zero visibility into financial performance, customer quality, or margin data.

The result?

Campaigns that look "wow!" and stroke your ego but drain your cash. Enquiries that go nowhere. Sales pipelines filled with the wrong people.

This is how good businesses lose months of momentum and tens of thousands in wasted cash.

The directors own the strategy

Let's set the record straight. Marketing strategy must come from the top.

Your remit is to make sure that every dollar spent on marketing has a gravitational pull to you. The greater the pull, the lower the push your sales team has to make, and that makes you more efficient. But more about that later…

It's the board, the business owners, and the CFO who hold the insight that matters:

- Which customers are most profitable
- Which products deliver the highest Gross Margin Dollars
- Which markets are growing, and which are changing
- What the real customer journey looks like from enquiry to payment

Only your leadership team has this full picture.

That's why they need to set the direction. Then your marketing team or agency can do what they do best: execute.

When leadership gives a clear remit to a great marketing team about exactly which customers, who are profitable and cashflow positive, to target, those teams deliver in spadefuls. They love the clarity. They run with it. The creative flows. The results show up fast.

You don't abdicate marketing strategy. You own it. Then you bring in the experts to bring it to life.

That's how you stop the tail from wagging the dog and stop burning through cash.

Lead quality over lead quantity

Here's where things turn around.

When you get your strategy right, your entire marketing engine starts targeting high-quality leads who

- want what you're selling,
- can afford to pay for it,
- understand your value, and
- pay you on time now (not someday).

And this has a direct impact on your cashflow. Because the better the customer, the faster the close, the healthier the margin, and the stronger your bank balance.

The core-customer engine

When you attract the right customer, you don't just close a sale, you open the door to sustainable, cash-generating growth.

We're going in deep, right where the real growth lives. These aren't surface-level hacks. These are proven, powerful tools I've used for decades to build businesses that scale with cash, not chaos. I know they work, hand on heart.

Something that gets overlooked far too often in business strategy is whom you sell to and how you position what you sell. It might sound simple. It's not. This is the foundation of a cashflow-positive business, one that funds its growth instead of relying on outside money to stay afloat. Nail this, and you stop chasing your tail. You start scaling with clarity, confidence, and cash in the bank.

What Bob Bloom got right

Bob Bloom, author of *The Inside Advantage*, nailed it. He defines your core customer as the person or company that you can serve repeatedly, profitably, and exceptionally well. The core customer also pays you on time, every time.

Think about that. Not just anyone who buys your product. The one who buys it, pays promptly, loves it, comes back for more, and tells others about it.

When you build your business around this customer, everything becomes easier. Your marketing gets clearer. Your sales process shortens. Your delivery becomes more predictable. And most importantly, your cashflow becomes more stable. Why? Because you're no longer wasting time and resources chasing the wrong people who don't or won't pay you on time. You're focused. You're aligned. You're efficient. And that's when things start to feel good.

The Hormozi effect: Crafting the "no-brainer" offer

Alex Hormozi, in *$100M Leads*, takes this concept even further. He argues that the most successful businesses create an offer so good, so well-targeted, that it feels like a no-brainer to the right customer. And it doesn't just stop at the offer, it's how you position it, how you package it, how you message it.

When you match your offer to your true core customer, you create what Hormozi calls an "offer vacuum". A gravitational pull that brings in high-quality leads, reduces friction in the sales process, and massively improves your closing rate.

And guess what happens when you consistently close the right customers at the right price? You improve your Gross Margin Dollars, you reduce (or eliminate) your churn, and you get paid faster. Because they are prioritising buying what you sell.

It's what they want and need.

You start creating real traction, the kind that feels less like a hustle and more like momentum.

Getting the core customer right: The cashflow impact

When you are laser-focused on your core customer and nail your offer vacuum, your business begins to operate like a well-oiled machine.

You're not stretching your delivery team to serve clients who aren't a fit. You're not discounting to close deals. You're not spending a fortune on marketing to the wrong audience. And it will be mind-blowingly true that your expensive sales team isn't wasting months persuading customers that your product is the best decision they can make. They're engaged with customers who understand your value and respect your terms.

That's when the magic happens.

You start to see cash in the bank. Predictable, reliable, stress-reducing cashflow. You start generating enough cash to reinvest, pay your team well, and grow with confidence. You start relying less on debt and investors because the business is funding itself. And that's the kind of growth that feels good because it's real, and you earned it.

It's addictive.

The path to sustainable scaling

Here's the part few people talk about: Scaling through self-generated cashflow is possible, and it's wildly exciting.

It means your product or service has found its place in the market. It means your messaging is landing. It means your operations are aligned. It means your customers aren't just buying once, they're staying, paying, and referring.

This is the model you want to build if you're in it for the long game. No constant capital raising. No giving away equity to stay alive. No running on fumes. Just a healthy, profitable, cash-rich business that knows exactly who it serves and why it wins.

Final word: Everything gets easier once you target your core customer

If you want to build a business that runs on its own steam, start here:

- Define your core customer, just as Bob Bloom recommends, with laser focus.
- Build a no-brainer, Hormozi-style offer that speaks directly to this customer's biggest need.
- Position your value clearly and unapologetically.
- Protect your Gross Margin Dollars and enforce your trading terms.

When you do this, your business becomes more than viable; it becomes *obscenely valuable.* It becomes a cashflow engine. And it gives you the freedom to scale on your terms, without compromise.

This isn't just smart. It's sustainable. And it's what separates just surviving from scaling by using your cashflow.

Kickass Cashflow Power Move #11

Never outsource or abdicate your strategic thinking. That's your job as a director or owner. You can get help, but always stay in the driver's seat because at the end of the day, you are the one who will live with the consequences of the decisions made.

"A sales team thrives when every person is in the right seat, not competing with their weaknesses but compounding their strengths. True leadership isn't about filling roles, it's about unlocking potential."

— Ryan Tuckwood, Founder & CEO,
SWISH Sales Coaching

DAY 12

Which Hat is Your Sales Team Wearing?

I'll never forget the CEO of a farming equipment business who looked me dead in the eye and said, "My sales team loves their 'Business Development Manager' title, but not one of them has landed a new client in three years."

So, what were they doing?

Answering phones. Quoting repeat orders. Filling out the order book. Not finding *new* clients, just taking care of the ones they already had. These weren't Finders. They were *Minders*, the relationship nurturers. He called them "glorified order-takers" who were being *rewarded* like Finders. And the result? Disappointing margin and cash erosion for the business.

Why? Because every time an existing customer placed an order, those BDMs earned full commission, even though the customer was already in the system. The business was paying *customer acquisition cost (CAC)* to customers it had already acquired.

Not all salespeople are created equal, and that's a good thing

If there's one mistake I see leaders make over and over again, it's assuming that all salespeople are cut from the same cloth.

They're not.

And if you try to manage them like they are, you'll waste time, money, and a whole lot of energy wondering why your sales aren't increasing and your cashflow feels like it's stuck in a ditch.

Let me be blunt: This chapter is about freeing you from that thinking for good.

Stop paying CAC for customers you already own

If your team is earning commissions on orders from existing clients without lifting a finger to bring in new ones, you're not rewarding performance; you're inflating their egos.

CAC is quietly eroding your gross margin. That's not sales growth. That's expensive account management. Get crystal clear on who earns commissions, when, and why. Otherwise, you're burning cash on autopilot.

Time to rethink sales roles

David Maister, legendary author of *Managing the Professional Services Firm*, nailed it when he said every professional service has four key hats:

- **Finders:** They love the hunt, the cold outreach, and chasing new deals.
- **Minders:** They nurture relationships and protect existing accounts.
- **Grinders:** They're your quote writers, proposal pros, and CRM wizards.
- **Sales Coaches:** They keep the team sharp and the metrics on track.

Every one of these roles has a place, but only if you assign the right expectations, the right key performance indicators (KPIs), and the right compensation structure.

Trying to turn a Minder into a Finder is like handing scuba gear to a hang-gliding enthusiast and expecting them to reach new heights. It's not going to end well.

The Challenger edge

Matt Dixon's *The Challenger Sale* and *JOLT Effect* added rocket fuel to this conversation. The best salespeople aren't just relationship managers; they *teach*, *tailor*, and *take control*. They help customers *think* differently about their problems. They challenge assumptions. They build urgency. And most importantly, they know how to close.

If you've got a Finder with Challenger instincts, do everything in your power to coach, retain, and reward them. They're your rainmakers.

But if you've got a team of loyal Minders or dependable Grinders, don't try to force them into Finder mode. Instead, *build your sales process like a relay team*. Finders generate leads, Minders nurture relationships, Grinders support the backend, and Sales Coaches, like orchestra conductors, bring it all together.

That's how you win.

What to do next:

- **Audit your sales team:** Who's a Finder, Minder, Grinder, or Coach? Be honest and let everyone know their role and play to their strengths.
- **Match KPIs to strengths:** Stop setting everyone the same targets.
- **Fix your commission plans:** Only pay commissions when an acquisition is earned.

- **Invest in coaching:** Teach Minders and Grinders how to support the cashflow goal.
- **Celebrate roles equally:** No more hero worship for just one sales style.

Final word: Play to win, not just to sell

When you start measuring the right people the right way and stop paying commissions for standing still, you stop bleeding cash and start building a system that scales.

This isn't about working harder. It's about getting smarter with who you hire, how you train, and what behaviour, activity, and results you reward.

You've got the team. You've got the tools. Now build the playbook.

Your cashflow depends on it.

Kickass Cashflow Power Move #12

Make sure every salesperson plays to their strengths and knows their role, and only pay commissions to those who have truly earned it.

DAY 13

Sales Teams Pay Attention: Cashflow is All in *Your* Timing

What did the band leader name his two daughters? Anna1, Anna2

When I worked in a stockbroking firm during university, the brokers huddled three times a day. First thing, pre-market, to get their heads in the game. Lunchtime, to share insights and keep morale high. And end of day, to debrief and prep for tomorrow. It wasn't fluff; it was ritual. It created rhythm and results.

That same approach works for any sales team. High-performing sales teams thrive on rhythm, energy, and accountability. The tighter the coordination, the faster the close, the clearer the pipeline, and the smoother the cashflow.

It's not just about leads – it's about the right transactions at the right time.

Your business could be swimming in leads, but if they don't convert into the right kind of transactions, protect margin, pay on time, and drive consistent revenue, they won't move the needle. They certainly won't help your cashflow.

To sharpen the focus of your sales team, it's important that you, and they, understand two essential acronyms: MQL and SQL.

- **Marketing qualified lead (MQL):** This is someone who has shown interest in your product or service by engaging in your marketing content. Maybe they downloaded a guide, filled out a form, or watched a webinar. They're curious, not committed.
- **Sales qualified lead (SQL):** Ready to buy, this individual will likely close the deal within the next 90 days, based on a reasonable forecast.

Your sales team needs to prioritise SQLs

That doesn't mean ignoring the rest. It means managing time wisely. I've seen too many salespeople get dazzled by big, shiny opportunities and lose sight of the qualified prospects sitting right in front of them.

The more confidence your team has around the timing of a close, the more accurate your cashflow forecasting will be. And that confidence comes from structure, focus, and discipline.

Build focus and momentum with daily huddles

Daily huddles are your greatest productivity weapon. These short, focused meetings keep the team aligned, motivated, and moving. Morning huddles should focus on pitch rehearsal, top-of-funnel strategy, and key objectives. Afternoon huddles are about progress checks, pivots, and celebrating the wins.

Make the sales process clear and visible

Sales teams often struggle with consistency. They underprice to win the deal, misread customer readiness, or get caught in negotiation traps that bleed time and margin.

That's where a clear, visible sales process changes everything.

Every team member should understand

- the exact steps in the sales process,
- the probability of closing at each stage, and
- how to track deals weekly by stage and momentum.

When you've got visibility, you can spot what's working and what's not. If deals keep stalling at the same point, that's a signal. Maybe your negotiation tactics need work. Maybe you're attracting the wrong leads. Maybe it's time to tighten the offer.

Support your team with a "Best Practice Playbook"

Now take it one step further: Give your sales team a tool they can rely on.

Create a Best Practice Playbook with

- proven talk tracks and objection-handling strategies,
- your most effective closing tactics,
- guidance on prioritising clients who pay quickly,
- upsell and cross-sell offers that improve cashflow,
- real-world examples, scenarios, and role-plays.

Make it accessible digitally or in print. Train on it regularly. And revise it often.

Your sales process is not set-and-forget. It should evolve with the market and with your team's insights. Encourage your salespeople to give feedback on what's working. Ask them what they're hearing from customers. Invite their input on pricing strategy. This does two things:

- It brings you real-time intel from the front lines.
- It supports a culture of inclusion, which drives buy-in and performance.

Why all of this matters for cashflow

When your sales team focuses on the right deals and works a clear, disciplined process, your business becomes predictable.

Cash comes in when you expect it. Gross Margin Dollars stays healthy. Sales don't just close; they close at the right time and with the right terms.

And that consistency is what allows you to:

- plan forward with confidence,
- fund growth without borrowing, and
- keep your team paid, your suppliers happy, and your stress levels down.

The head of sales owns cashflow forecasting

Yes, you read that right. It's not owned by the accountants; they're the scorekeepers. **Blaming the accountants for bad cashflow is like a football team blaming the scoreboard operator because they didn't score a goal. It doesn't make any sense.**

Cashflow forecasts are often wrong, not because finance teams can't do math, but because sales teams have "happy ears". They overestimate how soon a deal will close, or the likeliness of when it will land, if at all. That misjudgement throws everything off. Suddenly, the cash that the business counted on doesn't arrive on time, and now there's pressure. Cashflow is tight, you can't hire the next person you promised your ops team, you can't pay bonuses, and you can't open that new location.

And here's the kicker: It's not the finance team's fault. It's the sales team that controls when cash hits the bank. If they're committing to numbers without really understanding the implications of missing them, they're putting the whole business at risk and under stress.

A colleague of mine, Rob Monson, put it perfectly: "The cashflow forecast needs to be owned by the sales team, not the finance team".

And I second that idea. Because only when sales is accountable for the timing of both when the deal will close and when cash will land in the bank account do we stand a realistic chance of building forecasts that are tighter, smarter, and usable.

Key takeaways

The sales cycle is the heartbeat of your business. A skilled, strategic sales team keeps that rhythm strong. You'll see smart, sustainable growth, not hype, when they

- understand the difference between marketing qualified leads (MQLs) and sales qualified leads (SQLs);
- prioritise the timing and the closing of cashflow-positive leads;
- use daily huddles to stay sharp and aligned;
- follow a defined process;
- learn from a real, dynamic playbook; and
- let your head of sales own the cashflow forecast.

You won't just win more sales. You'll build a business that breathes cash.

A well-trained, well-led sales team doesn't just drive revenue. Your sales pros drive rhythm and cashflow. And that gives you the freedom and power to scale on your terms.

Kickass Cashflow Power Move #13

Train your head of sales to own the cashflow forecast, because they will coach the sales team to land the sales on time, as promised. And once they're ready, make sure to let the rest of the business know that head of sales owns it.

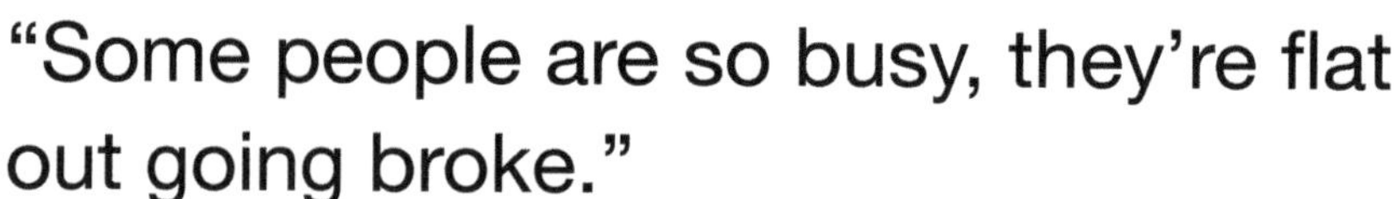

"Some people are so busy, they're flat out going broke."

— Paul Mackay, Managing Director, Miranda Auto Body

DAY 14

Shaken, Not Stirred: Your Cashflow Cocktail

There's a moment far too many entrepreneurs experience, when someone new joins the team, full of confidence and enthusiasm, and promises to take sales to a whole new level. They talk rapidly. They speak with conviction. They throw around buzzwords like "scale", "growth trajectory", and "volume strategy". And for a while, it's music to your ears.

That's exactly what happened to Stephen and Bella.

They had built their business the right way. Carefully. Intentionally. They offered services their clients truly valued, and they charged accordingly. Their business model was rooted in delivering high-margin work, which allowed them to grow steadily while maintaining excellent service and solid profits. There were no shortcuts. Just strong foundations, thoughtful decisions, and a team that understood how to serve well and make money doing it.

And then they decided it was time to expand.

They hired a new sales manager. He had the energy. He had the language. He looked and sounded like the person who could take them and their sales team to the next level. He pitched big ideas with ease, promising to flood the pipeline with deals and double revenue in six months.

Better still, the recruiter had headhunted him from one of the biggest players in the industry, so they believed everything that dropped out of his mouth was gold.

"We've got to scale," he told them. "Volume is everything."

He was convincing. Too convincing.

Stephen and Bella, despite their instincts, decided to hand over the reins of their sales strategy. That one decision, made with the best intentions, nearly cost them everything: the business, the house, and their marriage. Everything.

Within weeks, sales started pouring in. Sales climbed rapidly. On paper, everything looked fantastic. But underneath that surface-level success, the cracks were already forming. The deals were smaller. The Gross Margin Dollars was tighter. The clients were demanding, and their expectations were sky-high. The delivery team struggled to keep up. Fulfilment timelines stretched. Quality suffered.

The new salesperson demanded his comms EOM every month – double red flag!

It didn't take long before Bella raised the alarm.

"We haven't paid ourselves in weeks," she said.

Stephen's response was immediate and understandable, "We just need to sell more."

It's a common trap to believe that more sales are always the answer. But when the sales you're making are low-margin, high-effort, and misaligned with what your business does best, more is not better. It's just more pressure, more stress, and more financial strain.

Their business, once steady and thriving, was suddenly teetering on the edge.

They had fallen, in this cautionary tale, for what I like to call the "shiny sales trap", when someone comes in with flash and flair and derails everything you've built with a strategy that looks good on the outside but doesn't support the reality of your cashflow forecast.

Most of us are selling a mixed basket of products and services. And with that comes a mix of Gross Margin Dollars that gets blended to spit out a profit. This mixing adds to the complexity of truly understanding where the business is performing well and where it may be bleeding (as discussed on Day 7). All the team sees is that your sales figures are in the millions of dollars and you must be "raking it in". They don't understand the backstory… and that becomes dangerous for cashflow.

What saved them was a return to the basics. A return to the truth. During one of our Performance 7 Quarterly Advance planning sessions, they brought their focus back to margin-first selling. They reviewed every offer and identified which ones consistently delivered strong profitability.

That's when they realised their mistake. And to their credit, they didn't just keep pushing forward and hoping things would fix themselves. They hit pause. They regrouped. And they chose to rebuild their sales strategy from the ground up.

They rewrote their commission plan so that their sales team was rewarded not for volume alone, but for the right margin dollar deals that aligned with the business's financial goals. They retrained the team to understand the importance of selling what the company could deliver well and profitably. And perhaps most importantly, they started tracking margin contribution every single week. Not just sales. Not vanity metrics. Real numbers that reflected financial health. The new sales manager resigned, as he just couldn't handle how Stephen and Bella took back the reins of the business and changed the focus onto Gross Margin Dollars.

It didn't happen overnight. But it worked.

They started closing fewer deals, but the right ones. Their clients were a better fit. Their delivery team got back into their rhythm. Quality returned. And the money followed.

Sometimes, fewer sales are exactly what a business needs

The truth is, every business has a natural rhythm. A balance between what it sells, how it delivers, and how it grows. That rhythm is deeply connected to your cashflow, and the health of that cashflow is what allows you to sleep at night, invest wisely, and build something that lasts.

Here's where the cocktail analogy comes in.

Your business is like a well-crafted cocktail. Every offering you sell is an ingredient. Your high-margin services? That's your base spirit: strong, rich, foundational. The repeatable, reliable offerings? Those are your mixers: They add balance and make things scalable. And your strategic promos and one-off campaigns? Those are your garnishes: eye-catching, limited, and meant to elevate, not overwhelm.

Now, imagine throwing in low-margin, high-effort deals just for the sake of hitting volume. It's like dumping soda water into a premium cocktail just to fill the glass. It waters everything down. The flavour disappears. The strength is lost. And the experience? Forgettable.

Your product mix matters.

You don't need more ingredients. You need the *right* ones.

That's what Stephen and Bella rediscovered. And it changed everything.

There's a broader lesson here, too: Overselling isn't heroic. It's reckless. And it's avoidable.

Similar to marketing, when you let someone else dictate your sales strategy, especially someone who doesn't understand your numbers, your team, or your delivery capacity, you risk more than just a few bad deals. You risk the trust of your customers. The health of your operations. The spirit of your people. And your ability to lead with clarity.

It's easy to get swept up in energy and charisma. But in business, cash results are what matter. A confident pitch means nothing if it doesn't lead to sustainable, cashflow-positive, and profitable growth.

The answer isn't to stop growing. It's to grow with intention. To scale what works. To protect your delivery team. To know your numbers. To back your strategy with data, not just gut feel and certainly not just someone else's swagger.

Because here's the thing: You know more than you think you do.

You built this business. You've made good decisions before. And even when you've made missteps, you've learned from them. That's what makes you capable of leading your growth the right way.

So, if you're in a season where you're questioning your sales strategy or wondering whether that new hire really "gets it", this is your moment to pause and reassess.

Look at your product mix. Revisit your marginal cashflow. Ask if your sales efforts are aligned with your ability to deliver for cashflow excellence. And most of all, trust yourself.

Cash isn't just a financial measure. It's power. It's peace. It's the space to think clearly, to lead well, and to build a future you want to live.

Think of your offer suite as your cashflow cocktail: Designed with care. Built to strengthen your cash position and fund future growth. A measured mix with confidence. And always, perhaps, shaken, not stirred.

Kickass Cashflow Power Move #14

Don't take advice from anyone who doesn't understand the impact of product or service mix on cashflow dollars.

"Creativity is allowing yourself to make mistakes. Art is knowing which ones to keep."

— Scott Adams

DAY 15

Know the Real Cost of Acquiring a Customer

Last year, I started working with a husband-and-wife services business that, within two years, had quickly scaled to a team of 20 and $10 million in revenue. They brought me in to help them build profitability and align their team so they could scale interstate.

We got the company on track and built it to approximately $650,000 in profit… until they hired a new "superstar" salesperson (proudly headhunted from the competition) who quickly started selling all the wrong types of products to build revenue (and his commission).

The previous quarter, they were $500,000 cash up, but within four months of the new salesperson starting, ALL the cash was gone. They were broke, broken, and literally had no money for Christmas.

My husband Peter and I jumped in to help them identify the right product mix. We redirected the sales team to sell profitable and cashflow-positive sales. Long story short, they had a great Christmas, but geez, the going was tough.

That was not all of the bleeding, though. This business also had hired a marketing agency who was generating Facebook leads, but the cost per lead (CPL) was escalating and no one was tracking it until three weeks after month-end. What made things worse is that the leads generated were for work that was low-margin. When we added the CPL to the sales team's commissions to convert the lead and compared that to the gross margin, we found that the margin was less than the cost to acquire. We brought the leadership team together and walked them through some tools that helped them understand why their thinking of "we're selling heaps and really busy, the owner must be making a fortune!" was flawed. They saw the numbers, rallied around the owners, and turned the business around. It's now back on track and booming. Good people, a few tweaks, and an aligned team that supported the owners has now made this business a cash cow.

If my book can help more couples like this, I will be very happy.

I get why they found themselves struggling with cashflow. Marketing and sales teams are under massive pressure. They're expected to generate great leads cheap, close deals fast, hit revenue targets, and somehow make it all look easy. I've worked alongside enough teams to know that this work is demanding. So, what I'm about to say comes with deep respect:

If you don't know what it costs to acquire a customer, you're not in control of your growth or your cashflow.

CAC isn't just a metric for the finance team. It's a mirror. It reflects how efficiently your business turns interest into cash. Not leads. Not likes. Actual paying, bank-clearing, cash-in-the-door customers. And if your CAC is out of whack or worse, unknown, you might be scaling your way straight into a cashflow crunch.

A business with an efficient CAC has a significant cashflow advantage. Every customer acquired at a healthy cost strengthens your business's cashflow. But every dollar wasted on the wrong lead creates a cash gap that you'll feel burn.

Let's break this down with some real examples.

High-touch consulting business

You spend $15,000 a month on marketing, sales team wages, commissions, and a small marketing agency retainer. Together they win 10 new customers.

Your CAC is \$15,000 spend divided by 10 new customers. Each customer cost you \$1,500 to win. If each customer only generates \$1,200 in the first three months of working with your business then you're bleeding cash on every sale.

E-commerce business

You spend \$8,000 across ads, influencer fees, email tools, and creative. You acquire 160 new customers. CAC = \$50. If the average margin is \$120 and customers often return, that's a healthy CAC. You're building momentum without draining cash.

Here's your baseline formula:

CAC = Total sales and marketing spend
÷ number of new customers acquired

Let's get clear on what counts.

Total sales and marketing spend includes

- salaries and commissions for your sales team;
- ad spend, content creation, software, marketing agencies; and
- training, tools, events, and bonuses for every dollar that goes into acquisition.

New customers acquired = actual paying customers in that time frame (monthly or quarterly works best).

Here is a formula to help you do that:

LTV-to-CAC Ratio = Customer Lifetime Value ÷ CAC

Your target ratio should be: 3:1 or better. The bigger the better.

If your ratio is below that, you either need to reduce CAC, improve retention, or lift your average deal size fast. Because when that ratio falls apart, so does your ability to generate sustainable, self-funding growth.

Here's where most business owners get blindsided: They fall in love with sales numbers and forget to check the cost of getting there.

If it costs you $2,000 to land a customer who only brings in $1,500 margin (or value) over their lifetime, you're scaling backwards.

Efficient CAC buys you time, confidence, and cash. Inefficient CAC sinks your business slowly, burns your cash, and delays growth.

This is why CAC matters so much:

- It shows whether your growth is scalable.
- It tells you how to plan your marketing and sales budget with precision.
- It exposes whether you have a sales-efficiency or lead-quality problem.

When you know your CAC, you stop guessing. You start leading. And when it's efficient, you're not just growing. You're building a self-funding engine that keeps your cash flowing.

Here's an exercise that will bring this to life:

- Pull up your last three months of marketing and sales spend.
- Tally up your *new* paying customers.
- Run the CAC.
- Now, calculate your LTV.

When you've got both numbers, you're in a whole new position of power. You'll know which campaigns are leaking money and which ones to scale. You'll see clearly which customer segments are worth pursuing and which ones you need to let go.

You'll stop chasing the wrong sales volume and start building cash coffers.

Quick CAC Checklist: What to track monthly

- Total spend on sales and marketing (ads, salaries, commissions, tools)
- Number of new customers signed
- Average margin dollars per customer
- Customer retention (how long they stay)
- LTV-to-CAC ratio (aim for 3:1 or better)
- Breakeven timeline (when each customer becomes profitable)

Final word

Understanding your CAC is more than a marketing metric; it's a cashflow management tool. When you manage your CAC well, you manage your cash well. It's that simple.

Every decision you make around spend, scale, pricing, and customer targeting flows downstream into your bank account. Nail your CAC, and you create reliable, repeatable, cash-generating growth. Get it wrong, and you'll constantly feel like you're catching up, burning through runway, deferring decisions, or chasing capital.

So, use your CAC as a lever, not just a number. Use it to

- guide your growth,
- build something sustainable, and
- scale on your terms with profit, with purpose, and with money in the bank.

Kickass Cashflow Power Move #15

Know and track your CAC per product or service.

“Experience Italy with every bite, and make it a habit.”

— Every successful Italian restaurant owner, ever.

DAY 16

Lifetime Value of a Customer

Too many business owners are obsessed with the chase. New ads, new promos, new customers. Sure, landing a fresh face feels like a win, but if that's all you're focused on, you're working twice as hard for half the reward.

The truth? The first sale is just the first deal's handshake. The real Kickass Cashflow show happens when that customer keeps coming back.

That's what we call the **lifetime value of a customer**. And here's the key:

$$V = \textit{Gross Margin Dollars}$$

Not revenue. Not vanity numbers. Only margin counts, because that's what fuels your cashflow.

Arthur & Rene's Café

We're going to look at a simple case study, one that I know all of you can relate to.

Meet Arthur & Rene, a husband-and-wife team running a bustling suburban café. They've built something special: a cozy place where locals gather for caffeine, chats, and croissants.

But behind the smiles? Stress.

They're spending money on local ads, specials, and café apps, hoping to drag in new walk-ins. A customer spends $28 on a meal, they pocket about $20 in profit, and… poof. That's it. At the end of the month, bills loom, payroll's tight, and they feel like hamsters on a wheel.

Now, let's flip the script.

Here are their real numbers:

- **Average spend:** $28
- **Margin:** 70% → $19.60 profit per visit
- **Frequency:** 3 visits a week = 156 per year
- **Customer lifespan:** 3 years on average

$$LTV = Gross\ Margin \times Frequency \times Lifespan$$
$$= \$19.60 \times 156 \times 3$$
$$= \$9{,}172.80$$

Let that sink in.

One loyal café customer isn't worth $20. They're worth over *nine grand in cashflow* over three years.

Arthur & Rene didn't need more ads. They needed to realise they were sitting on a goldmine: regulars who, if nurtured, became $9,000 assets instead of one-off transactions.

Lifetime value (LTV) isn't a fluffy marketing metric, it's a *cashflow booster*. It shows you where the cash will come from in the future.

Here's why it matters:

- **It reveals the truth:** You're not guessing, you know what each customer is really worth to your bottom line.
- **It highlights your VIPs:** Not every customer is equal. LTV shows you who deserves the red-carpet treatment.
- **It stabilises your cashflow:** No more starting from zero every month. You've got steady, predictable income rolling in.

Your LTV Playbook

Here's how to turn one-time buyers into repeat-profit machines:

Step 1: Calculate LTV

Use the formula:

$$LTV = Gross\ Margin\ Dollars \times Purchase\ Frequency \times Customer\ Lifespan$$

Gross Margin Dollars is key. Revenue is the dumbest number on the planet to focus on.

Step 2: Boost frequency

Arthur & Rene introduced a simple loyalty card: Buy nine coffees, get the tenth free. Suddenly, weekly visitors doubled their trips. Regulars lingered longer and ordered food.

Step 3: Extend lifespan

Keep customers longer by making them feel like family. Arthur & Rene learned people loved hearing, "Melanie, Flat white, extra hot, right?" That little recognition kept them loyal.

Step 4: Protect margin

Stop handing out endless discounts. Arthur & Rene swapped "10% off breakfast" for upsells, "Would you like a bottle of water with that latte?" Same customers, more margin dollars.

The shift

When Arthur & Rene stopped chasing strangers and started doubling down on their regulars, everything changed.

Payroll stopped being a nail-biter.

Suppliers got paid without frantic calls.

And for the first time in years, they took a family holiday without checking their bank balance three times a day.

That's the power of LTV. It doesn't just grow your business, it *stabilises* it. It gives you options, breathing room, and confidence.

Perhaps a simple example, but I know you'll resonate. The question is "what processes are you going to build so that you ensure repeat purchases in your business?"

Kickass Cashflow Power Move #16

Super profits live in repeat business. Treat your regulars like the $9,000 assets they are and train your team to see loyalty as the ultimate cashflow strategy.

SECTION 3

Growth Sucks Cash: Don’t Let Ego Run the Show

Growth demands cash. Full stop.

Every time a business scales, it increases pressure on working capital. Payroll expands. Supplier orders increase. Operating expenses rise. There are more zeros everywhere you look. There are more transactions, and each one moves larger sums of money. The stakes get higher, and the margin for error gets tighter.

But here's the truth most business owners avoid: Ego often drives growth faster than cashflow can support it. It's easy to fall into the trap of chasing visual validation, more staff, bigger offices, flashier tools, higher sales targets, without fully understanding the financial strain it creates behind the scenes.

The internet doesn't help. Social media feeds are full of noise from entrepreneurs selling the dream, flaunting revenue milestones, and celebrating "scale" without any visibility into whether the business is actually profitable or sustainable. Don't get distracted. Revenue is not reality. Cash is.

I work inside boardrooms. I see the P&Ls, the balance sheets, the live bank feeds. I know the numbers. And I can tell you this with full confidence: Real wealth is calm, deliberate, and in control. It doesn't need to prove anything. It doesn't need to rush. It plans its growth, funds it properly, and protects margin along the way. True wealth walks in quiet confidence, not loud performance.

Cashflow-positive business growth is beautiful when done right.

But ego-led growth is a wrecking ball to your bottom line.

When you scale, your costs don't just increase, they compound. You pay more people, you carry more stock, you wait longer for debtors to pay, and you take on bigger risk with every decision. Growth is not a vanity metric. It's a financial responsibility. Scaling your business is a bold move. But if your cashflow doesn't grow with it, you create fragility, not freedom.

Let's grow the smart way. Strategic, profitable, cashflow-positive growth. Nothing less.

Let's get to work.

“It’s moments like these that force us to try harder, and dig deeper, and to discover gifts we never knew we had. To find the greatness that lies within each of us.”

— Barack Obama

DAY 17

Valley of Death: Understanding the Double Dip Curve

If I had a dollar for every time someone thought scaling means adding more headcount, I'd be Elon Musk rich. Scaling your business isn't about hiring more people, leasing bigger offices, or throwing money at every shiny software that promises efficiency. Real growth is about *building margin dollars*, not ballooning your overheads.

Yet too many business owners confuse headcount with progress and size with success. And in doing so, they set themselves up for a cashflow crisis that quietly drains their business from the inside out.

Do not let your ego blow up your business's cashflow.

In the words of Greg Crabtree, your overheads are the silent killer of profitability. You can't fix cashflow by selling more if your operational engine is leaking money from every bolt.

The truth about overheads

Overheads are the costs you incur to run your business, but they're not directly tied to delivering your product or service. We're talking admin salaries, rent, software subscriptions, utilities, insurance, management bonuses, coffee pods, and the Friday team drinks that somehow became sacred, *every* Friday.

Now, none of these are bad on their own. But when left unchecked? They grow like weeds. And unlike COGS, which scales up and down with sales, overheads just *sit there*. Constant. Fixed. Waiting to be paid, no matter what your sales are doing.

When you're riding high, overheads feel manageable. But the minute when sales dip, projects are delayed, or customers pay late? That overhead load becomes a cash drain.

Overhead creep: How it happens

No one wakes up and says, "Let's make our business inefficient today." Overhead creep is slow. Subtle. It happens when you

- hire an extra admin because someone's overloaded;
- add new software without retiring the old one;
- rent a bigger space "for future growth";
- create layers of management instead of systems, also known as "throwing bodies at the problem"; and
- buy tools, programs, and consultants that don't get fully utilised.

All of it feels justified in the moment. But collectively? It eats away your net profit. It raises your breakeven point. It demands more sales just to cover the same ground. And when you're constantly chasing revenue just to stay still, your business is under stress, not scaling.

The real cost of a bloated back office

A $1 million business with $700,000 in overheads and $300,000 in COGS is not lean. It's inefficient.

You might look like you're growing. But underneath the surface, you're funding inefficiency with every invoice. You're not building a business that breathes. You're building one that pants.

A bloated back office drains cash, kills agility, and forces you to compromise when things get tight. You cut the wrong things. You stop marketing. You underpay your delivery team. And that's how businesses start to crumble from the core.

The Valley of Death: Mistaking headcount for scale

Here's where it gets dangerous. Business owners get excited about growth. They see new work on the horizon and immediately jump to hiring, often in the form *of indirect labour*. Coordinators. Managers. Ops roles. They do it with the best of intentions: "I'm getting ahead of the curve. I'm preparing to scale."

But scaling isn't about adding layers of overhead. Scaling is about creating leverage. If you invest in indirect headcount before revenue has caught up, you enter what I call the *Valley of Death, Mark II.*

We're all aware of the innovation cycle's Valley of Death, where you invest heavily in developing a new product and bringing it to market. The Valley of Death refers to that white-knuckle moment when there's a gap between idea (cash spent to develop) and commercialisation (i.e., selling and money coming in).

But there's often a deeper dip to this Valley when businesses simultaneously spend on overheads to prepare for growth.

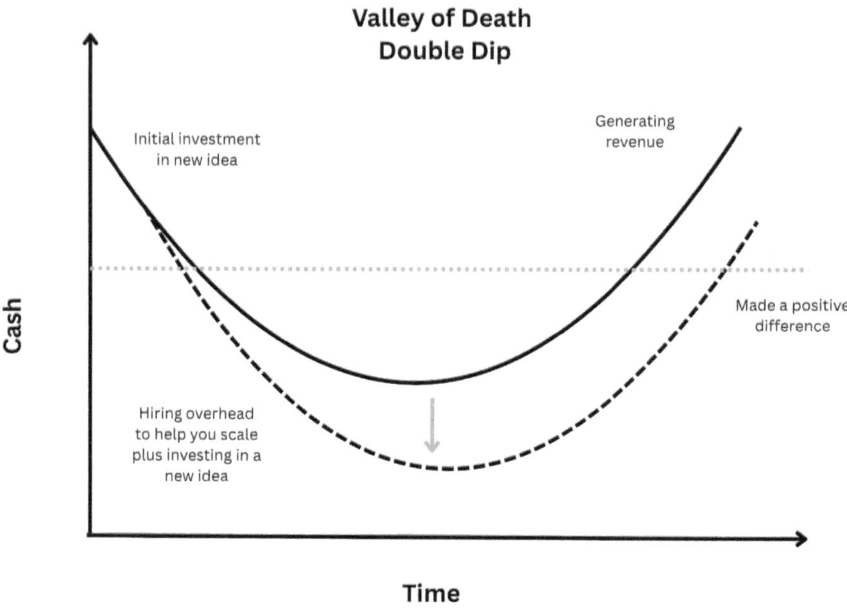

Figure 8: Double Dip Valley of Death

This is the runway between when you invest in people and when those people start generating a return. It's a white-knuckle phase where your cash reserves drop, your payroll spikes, and your marginal cashflow hasn't caught up.

If you're not prepared for it with a clear cashflow plan, financial buffer, and performance KPIs then you'll start to worry and make panicked decisions. You'll question your strategy, doubt your leadership, and potentially walk away just before the payoff arrives.

So yes, *invest in overhead* if the goal is to unlock future growth. But go in with eyes wide open. Know that there will be tense moments when cash dips. That's expected. But if your team hits their KPIs and your strategy holds, you *will* work through the crunch.

Crabtree's lens on overhead ratios

Greg Crabtree offers a brilliant tool for keeping overheads in check: *target ratios*. He suggests that your overheads should be *no more than 30% of revenue* in most small-to-mid-sized businesses. That means for every $1m you earn, your overheads shouldn't exceed $300,000. It's only a rule of thumb, but less overhead is best.

Too often, business owners justify high spending with a future promise: "This will help us scale. We need to invest in the future." But if it's not driving immediate efficiency or freeing up revenue-generating capacity, it's not leverage, it's cash lag.

Here's a quick gut check:

- Is this cost helping me generate more margin?
- Is it helping my team deliver faster or better?
- Is it removing friction between the sales and delivery teams?
- Is it creating a wow customer experience so we increase repeat purchases?

If not? It needs scrutiny.

How to audit your overhead like a pro

- **List all recurring expenses:** software subscriptions, mobile phones plans, rent, utilities, admin salaries, insurance, etc.
- **Categorise by function:** admin, marketing, finance, HR, leadership.
- **Attach ROI:** What does each line item help you *do better or faster*?
- **Ask the tough questions:** Would you sign up for it *today* if it wasn't already in place? Have some underperforming team members overstayed on your payroll?

Also, look at the *overlap*. Are you paying three tools to do one job? Are people duplicating work that could be automated or streamlined?

These are signs that your business engine is misfiring.

Overhead should serve delivery, not distract from it

Here's the mindset shift: Overhead should *support* your delivery engine, not compete with it. In fact, in my world **overheads are referred to as Accelerators.**

Every overhead cost should:

- protect the quality of your product,
- increase the speed or efficiency of delivery,
- create leverage for more revenue, and
- support the sales and delivery team to service customers faster.

If it doesn't, then it's not strategic. It's just dead weight.

What to do before you hire another overhead role

- **Map the work:** Is it repeatable? Is it predictable?
- **Systemise it first:** Can a tool or process reduce the load?
- **Assign it temporarily:** Test the need before you commit long term.
- **Tie it to a KPI:** What will success look like within 90 days?

If that role doesn't free up margin, speed, or capacity, you're just adding cost. And that cost will become a cash outflow whether cash inflows from sales show up or not.

Profit and cashflow are not an accident.

The hidden weight of growth: When new ideas and overhead become cashflow killers

Overhead as you scale is not destiny. It's a choice. And just like pricing, it's a lever you control.

Businesses that thrive don't just focus on top-line revenue. They obsess over margin dollars. They build lean, focused teams. They measure every cost by its contribution to delivery, margin, and momentum.

So, the next time you think growth means adding another layer of support staff, ask yourself: *Is this a growth lever or a cash drain?*

Because kickass cashflow doesn't happen by accident. It's the outcome of strategic decisions made with discipline, clarity, and courage.

Don't scale for show. That's a short-term strategy that leads to immense pain and pressure.

Ruthlessly persecute all overheads. Invest only in Accelerators, and give them clear direction, support, and coaching.

That's how you create a business that doesn't just grow, but one that stays cashflow strong in the good times and survives the hard ones too. Cash fuels optionality and leverage, the ultimate growth superpower.

Kickass Cashflow Power Move #17

Determined leaders don't fear the Valley of Death; they navigate it with cashflow discipline and overhead control at every turn.

SECTION 4

The WC Buckets

Boom! Smackdown the Slow Payers

Friends Don't Let Friends Miss a Payment

You Bought Too Much CRaP!

The WIP Ain't in Your Wallet

Yes, I know, the WC pun is intentional. But… WC stands for working capital.

The difference between cashflow and profit is often due to the way working capital is managed. Working capital, which includes stock on hand and accounts receivable and payable, ties up cash in the short term, affecting your cashflow even if your business is profitable.

Working capital impacts cashflow because it represents temporarily unavailable cash, creating a gap between profitability and actual cash on hand.

“Everything you want is just outside your comfort zone.”

— Robert Allen

DAY 18

Boom! Smackdown the Slow Payers

I worked with a consultancy that ran brilliant sales strategy workshops. They had elite clients, big-brand logos and $800k/month in invoiced revenue. But here's what no one saw: $1.2m was tied up in accounts receivable (AR).

They were paying a team of 12 consultants, plus ops, plus tech tools, every fortnight like clockwork. But their clients? They took 60, 75, even 90 days to pay. The founders were scrambling to find the cash to make payroll.

We changed two things:

- Introduced 30% deposits upfront for all new work.
- Assigned a dedicated AR enforcer (a take-no-hostages operator with polite persistence and nerves of steel).

Within 90 days, receivables dropped by 60%, payroll stress disappeared, and the founders finally paid themselves again.

If you're not getting paid on time, you're the one being played

Let's be blunt: When your clients pay late, you become their bank. No interest. No thanks. Just late. And while they enjoy the ROI from your work, you're left scrambling to make payroll, dipping into overdrafts, and losing sleep.

This is where so many entrepreneurs mess it up. They obsess over sales and overlook collections. But when sales don't convert to cash, then that's a mirage.

If you're going to survive, let alone scale, you need cash in the door. Not vibes. Not invoices. Not a promise after an excuse after ghosting. You need *cash*.

Fix your cash conversion game

Here's how late payments kill your cashflow:

You're paying staff weekly or fortnightly. So, money is dropping out of your bank account. You're billed for tools and freelancers monthly. But your clients? They're waiting 30, 60, 90 days to drop money into your bank account. That's a recipe for disaster. When you're a small business, you're owed perhaps $50-100k and somehow you manage to weather the storm with credit cards and a small overdraft for backup.

As you scale, however, a lot more zeros get added to your debtors, because you are invoicing a lot more every month. The banks and credit cards will cover you when there are a couple of zeros in debtors, but once you add five or six zeros to the amount owing, you need a different conversation. What worked when you were small won't work as you scale. And the game needs to change.

When cash at the bank is dwindling, often leaders lose their confidence, thinking that their business is tanking due to their team's poor performance. Yet when you run the calculation on the cash numbers, you realise that you're not inefficient. You're just not getting paid. It's as simple as that.

And you need to change things up if you're going to survive the next growth spurt.

So, here's how to win:

- *Get paid upfront.* Deposits are your new best friend. Don't start work until the money clears.
- *Lock in credit card or direct deposit payments.*
- If you can't get paid upfront, then *significantly shorten your trading days.*
- *Tie billing to milestones.* Break big projects into payment checkpoints and make progress claims.
- *Tighten your terms.* No more 30-day silliness. Go for 7 or 14 days. If they want 30+, charge them for the generosity.
- *Automate follow-up.* Reminders go out at 7, 14, and 21 days. Then it's polite emails and calls. Then it's collections.

And most importantly: Hire or empower a killer AR person. This is the unsung hero in a cash-strong business. They're not just chasing money. They're building really strong relationships with your customers' admin team. That essentially protects your team by making sure you can consistently make payroll and fuel your growth. Your AR person is your secret weapon.

What to do this week:

- **Audit your AR balance:** How much are you owed right now?
- **Segment your clients:** Who pays late? Who pays fast? Who needs to go?
- **Rewrite your terms:** Start with new clients. 50% upfront, balance on delivery.
- **Build a follow-up process:** Make it automated, polite, and persistent. Like I mean, really persistent… to the point of super annoying.
- **Find or assign a Debtors' Champion:** Give them authority and a bonus for results.

Cash in the bank beats hopes in the inbox

When you clean up accounts receivable, everything shifts.

You stop second-guessing your cashflow. You start planning hires, expansion, and innovation. You stop reacting and start building.

There is nothing more powerful than a business that delivers value and gets paid like clockwork.

This is your power move. Your line in the sand. Your cash is not a negotiation. You did the work; you deserve to be paid. For me, it's all about respect.

Make it happen.

You don't need more hustle. You need to get paid.

Let's go.

Kickass Cashflow Power Move #18

Chasing debtors is so last season; stop burying your head in the sand and build a process to deal with this once and for all.

“Distance means so little, when someone means so much.”

— Tom McNeal

DAY 19

Friends Don't Let Friends Miss a Payment

Pay like a pro and you'll never run dry

Cashflow isn't just about who owes you; it's also about who *you* owe. And if you treat your suppliers like afterthoughts, they'll remember.

Here's the kicker that most founders forget: Your accounts payable (AP) habits say everything about your character as a business. Pay fast, pay fair, and build trust, and you'll have options when it matters most.

In a crunch, people move mountains for people they respect. Especially the quiet heroes in accounts receivable.

High tea, loyalty, and supply chain gold

Let me tell you about Lucy.

Lucy wasn't flashy. She didn't sit in strategy meetings or pitch investors. But Lucy ran the accounts payable desk like a boss. She managed payments for a mid-sized national manufacturer and distributor business in the health and wellness sector.

When COVID hit and supply chains crumbled, panic spread. No one could get the stock and key ingredients. Containers were stuck in ports. Admin teams at suppliers were drowning in demand and debt.

But not Lucy.

Her inbox stayed open. Her phone line was direct. And she had what no one else had: *loyalty*.

For the three years prior, Lucy had cultivated real relationships with every supplier's AR team. She learned their kids' names. She knew who loved shortbread and who loved gin. And twice a year? She loved to spoil them.

Not just polite emails. Not just holiday cards. High tea. Champagne. Connection.

For the international suppliers, Lucy sent all her AR colleagues an Aussie gift basket with Vegemite, Tim Tams, Australian wines, and a beach towel.

When she first pitched this to her boss, she balked. "We're taking supplier admin to high tea?" Lucy didn't flinch. "If they like us, we get what we need when it matters most."

And she was right.

When demand outstripped supply in July 2020 and customers were clawing for product, Lucy made one call and secured priority dispatch. Even for critical ingredients that "were out of stock", Lucy could get her hands on what was needed. Every time. While competitors were taking out emergency loans to cover massive inventory stockpiles for orders that had missing parts and they couldn't complete, Lucy's business *boomed*.

Why? Because she paid on time, showed up with generosity, and treated AR like the strategic team they are.

The year after things settled down, Lucy approached her boss again and asked for more funds. This time it wasn't for high tea; it was for Taylor Swift tickets so she could take her key AR strategic partners out for a treat. And she got the funds.

Make AP a relationship power tool

Accounts payable isn't just about when the bills go out; it's also how you use that loyalty to build leverage.

Here's how to do it like Lucy:

- **Know your suppliers' AR teams by name:** Learn who they are, what matters to them.
- **Always pay on the day you said you would:** Not early, not late. *Exact.*
- **Send confirmation notes when payments are made:** Never leave them guessing.
- **Build connections outside of a crisis:** Frequent "just because" catch-ups, thank you calls, and even small gifts.
- **Celebrate reliability:** If a supplier consistently delivers for you, let their AR team know it.

The real trick?

Budget for nurturing relationships.

Just like you fund marketing or sales dinners, set aside money to build goodwill. A $1,000 high tea expense might save you $50k in stock you didn't miss when the world flipped upside down.

Build your supplier loyalty program this quarter

Great supplier relationships don't happen by accident. Putting the right systems in place will help the cause:

- **Create a supplier contact map:** Who are the AR people behind your top 10 vendors?
- **Schedule a quarterly check-in:** Nothing formal. Just a human-to-human conversation.

- **Set a payment promise policy:** Make it clear internally: We pay when we say we will.
- **Design your goodwill plan:** High tea? Coffee vouchers? Holiday hampers? Pick something, or even better – pick three!
- **Track and reward reliability:** Create a "supplier of the quarter" award and include their AR team.

Paying on time buys you options

In the world of business, *goodwill is a currency*. And Lucy proved it.

While her competitors were pleading for stock and begging banks for loans, she was getting next-day shipping and "we'll hold a pallet just for you" phone calls.

Want to future-proof your business? Build real relationships with the people behind the spreadsheets.

Because when the pressure hits, the people who get looked after are the ones who have always shown up. Not the loudest. Not the biggest. The *most reliable.*

Pay with consistency. Lead with gratitude. Build supplier friendships that money can't buy.

That's how you win the long game.

Kickass Cashflow Power Move #19

Nurture your supplier relationships like Lucy. Loyalty is earned before the crisis hits.

“A clean house is a sign of a well-run life.”

— Unknown

DAY 20

You Bought Too Much CRaP!

Meet Josh. Josh was offered a cracker of a deal by his supplier: Buy 12 months' worth of stock, get a 10% discount. On a $500,000 order, that looked like a $50,000 saving. Josh jumped in; he thought he had big opportunity to make some fast money. Six months later, he was still sitting on $450,000 of stock that nobody wants because the supplier changed the packaging. To make matters worse, he borrowed to fund the deal, so he was paying interest on dead stock – double ouch! When cutting the deal with the supplier, he also negotiated a $40,000 rebate, but only if the stock sold within 12 months. He missed that too. What looked like a $90,000 win has turned into a $450,000 cash trap, sitting in his warehouse, $40,000 rebate lost, plus interest bleeding away each month.

This is what happens when you Can't Realise any Profit (CRaP). Inventory that doesn't sell is a cash muncher. It could be a bad decision, obsolete stock, a product that's gone out of fashion, or simply that a better version now exists. Either way, the result is the same: You don't just miss out on the opportunity to bank a profit, you strangle your cashflow. Josh thought he was saving $50,000. In reality, he buried nearly half a million dollars in product that's gathering dust.

The lesson: Discounts don't equal profit if you can't turn the stock into cash.

Test the deal before you buy

Before jumping on a supplier discount, ask yourself three questions:

- Will the product sell in the timeframe I need?
- What is the real cash cost if I hold this stock (financing, storage, rebate conditions)?
- Am I buying profit, or am I just tying up cash?

If the answer to the last question is "tying up cash", walk away. A discount is worthless if the stock doesn't move quickly.

If it's just sitting there, it's stealing from you

Let's talk truth: Every box of unsold stock sitting on your shelves is robbing your business of opportunity. That's your money, it's your potential boxed up, doing nothing. While you're hustling to grow, your warehouse is throwing shade on your cashflow.

You thought you were being smart, right? Stocking up so you'd "never run out." But now you're looking at pallets of products that feel more like anchors than assets.

Slay the inventory drain like a queen

You don't need less ambition; you need smarter inventory.

Here's how to handle it like Mel Robbins with Rihanna's don't-mess-with-me attitude:

- **Know your stock turns:** If it doesn't sell at least 3-4 times a year, ditch the bulk orders.
- **Track carrying cost like a boss:** Every week that product sits, it's costing you shelf space, energy, and flexibility.
- **Keep expiry top of mind:** Whether it's actual dates or shelf-life, trends and formulas change fast.

- **Bulk is a trap if it doesn't move:** That 15% discount isn't worth a 12-month headache.
- **Only say yes to rebates you'll collect:** Then assign a Rebate Champion to make sure you do.

A word of warning

Don't let the sales team lead your demand planning, because they have happy ears. They love ordering heaps of stock so they can fulfill orders. But the reality is that they rarely ever sell everything they have ordered, and you end up with a shed full of obsolete stock, aka cash on the shelf.

Out-of-stocks are a mixed blessing, and as the business grows, you need to be all over this stock level. Too much and your cash is hamstrung. Too little and your sales team and customers lose confidence that you can deliver on time.

Setting clear expectations upfront is a leadership standard of excellence that you, as the owner, need to set. Otherwise, your cashflow will be in pain.

Five moves to stop the stock suck

Take an active approach to staying on top of your stock. Technology can be your friend, so make sure you use it.

- **Run your aged stock report:** Highlight anything that's been sitting longer than 90 days.
- **Track every rebate offer:** Tie it to product, sales goals, and timelines.
- **Stop letting suppliers run your warehouse:** Review every deal with a "Does this spark cashflow happiness?" lens.
- **Create a rebate collection system:** Automate what you can. Put one sharp operator on it.
- **Revise your buying strategy:** Order based on customer's demand, not pressure.

Stock that doesn't sell is cash you can't touch

Every box you bought on faith, every deal you took because "it felt smart", and every rebate you forgot to collect is part of the reason your cashflow feels tight.

Start treating your inventory like cash, because that's exactly what it is.

Don't let it sit. Move it. Don't get seduced. Stay sharp. And don't just buy what looks like a good deal. *Buy what makes your cashflow boom.*

You're not here to hoard. You're here to make money.

Kickass Cashflow Power Move #20

Cashflow kings and queens don't hoard. They rotate, reinvest, and reign.

“Time is money, but only if you collect it.”

— Every badass business owner, ever.

DAY 21

The WIP Ain't in Your Wallet

Back when Pete and I were running our accounting firm, we saved everything on paper. Client files lived in Manila folders and lever arch binders. One afternoon, when it was just the two of us left in the office, I noticed the floor was covered in neatly arranged client folders. They weren't filed away. They weren't delivered and closed. They were grouped by client in quiet little piles.

I asked Pete, "What's with all the files on the floor?"

He looked at me and said, "That's all our cash."

I didn't get it.

He said, "Every one of those files is a job we can't finish because we're waiting on one tiny piece of missing information from the client. And until we finish the job, we can't send out the bill. But we've already paid the team to do the work."

That was our work in progress (WIP). Our stock. Our cash. Sitting on the floor.

There was more than $180,000 of unbilled work scattered across the carpet, just waiting for a reply. The team had asked clients for the info, but no one was actively chasing. No urgency. Just limbo.

It shocked me.

The next morning, we created a plan to contact every client and send interim invoices. We were worried we'd upset people. But if the team had done the work, and the client hadn't responded to the queries, then we were sending an interim account to keep us cashflow positive.

Work in progress = Cash in handcuffs

If you're a professional service firm, your version of inventory isn't stacked in a warehouse; it's parked on time sheets. It's half-finished deliverables. It's unbilled strategy decks and client work that no one's invoiced yet.

And here's the kicker: that "work in progress"? It's your *cashflow kryptonite.*

WIP is to consultants, accountants, lawyers, architects, and marketers what dusty stock is to a wholesaler. It *feels* profitable. But it's cash that hasn't landed. Yet your team? Still getting paid. Your rent? Still due. Your cashflow runway? Shrinking.

Files on the floor and $180k on pause

Back when Pete and I were still using Manila folders, invoices were posted at month-end, with 30-day terms. That was the industry standard. Eventually, we shifted to 12 monthly instalment payments (an annual subscription model) with all clients. It smoothed our cashflow *and* theirs. Game-changer.

When service firms tell me they don't have any stock, I ask them to think again. To us, it's WIP, and it's a real cash drain if you're not careful. You need to be all over it and chase it.

Busy does not equal banked.

Bank the work by billing it

WIP needs rules. Systems. And a little rockstar discipline.

Here's how you fix it:

- **Shorten your billing cycle:** Don't wait for project completion. Bill in milestones. Bill weekly. Make "increase your billing frequency" your new daily affirmation.
- **Assign a WIP hawk:** Someone who scans active jobs every Friday and flags what's ready to invoice.
- **Automate timesheets:** No timesheet, no pay day (brutal, I know... but it works).
- **Train your team to think in "billable milestones":** Avoid billing for "perfect packages".
- **Make billing emotional:** Every dollar you don't bill this week is taking away from *your team's Bali Conference Fund*. Make it fun and watch everyone make it a priority.
- **Job profitability:** Keep track of your profitability (weekly is best). Nip problems in the bud.

The WIP ka-ching

Reducing WIP means cash in the bank. Here are five actionable steps to take now:

- **Audit your current WIP:** How many jobs are more than 50% done but unbilled?
- **Find the top 5 oldest jobs:** Ask one question: Why haven't we invoiced this?
- **Create a WIP-to-cash target:** Commit to reducing WIP by 30% this month.
- **Build a WIP dashboard:** Make progress (and pain) visible.
- **Reward billing speed:** If someone helps close WIP fast, they get a bonus. Period.

Cashflow loves speed

You already did the work. Now send the invoice.

In service firms, cash doesn't lag because of slow sales. It lags because of the slow conversion from payroll dollars out and client dollars in. That lag should be your obsession, like it was mine.

Final word: Scheduling of your team and efficient utilisation

We know this: **Cashflow loves billable hours**. When your team is on payroll five days a week but only two of those days are billable, the other three are gone. That's cash out the door with nothing coming back. You've paid for the hours, but they didn't earn a single dollar. In service firms, this is called utilisation. And here's the truth: Wasted hours are wasted cash; it's cash that's left your account and will never be seen again.

Here are two ways to flip the script:

- **Keep your team tightly scheduled:** Every hour planned is an hour that can be billed.
- **Flood yourself with demand:** Stack your pipeline so full you need a waitlist. A waitlist is pure cashflow power – it keeps your team billable, your business in control, and your cashflow bubbling like champagne.

Schedule tightly like a beast. Invoice frequently. Collect fast.

Kickass Cashflow Power Move #21

Cashflow gold is in tight schedules and peak utilisation. Work smarter, bank bigger. Flood yourself with demand, build a waitlist.

SECTION 5

Building Your Kickass Cashflow Team

We have no passengers on the leadership team.

Everyone is an A-Player and active participant in driving the business's success.

DAY 22

Your Kickass Leadership Team

Fire fast, hire legends: Your bank account will thank you.

One of my clients in the construction industry came to me stuck in a cycle of late jobs, stretched cash, and team fatigue. The business was growing on paper, but profit wasn't landing in the bank. They had skilled trades on site, but chronic miscommunication between supervisors, the estimating team, and project management meant everything ran late and over budget. The real issue? Their team was full of well-intentioned B-Players who lacked the horsepower to drive accountability.

We introduced an approach from the *Topgrading* hiring and recruiting platform: Every role got a clear scorecard. Site supervisors had measurable KPIs tied to job delivery dates, quality, and cost control. We restructured the hiring process, switching from gut instinct to structured interviews, and within six months, they'd replaced 40% of their operational team.

The result? Projects ran closer to schedule, margin variance tightened, and their project cashflow improved across the next three quarters. But the real game-changer? The owners stopped firefighting and started leading. With A-Players in place and clear KPIs, they finally had a business that performed without their constant intervention.

Brad Smart, in his groundbreaking work *Topgrading*, defined an A-Player as "someone who is in the top 10% of talent available for the role, at the remuneration level you're offering, in your specific market."

The percentage of A-Players in your business directly correlates with your cash position. Yes, I mean your bank account. If you're tired of cashflow stress, team drama, and putting out fires all day, then it's time to take a long, hard look at who's sitting on your team bus and whether they're driving you to growth or dragging you into the red.

That definition isn't just theory: It's a lens that separates high-growth businesses from those that are stuck on the hamster wheel of hiring the wrong people over and over again.

Don't confuse A-Players with prima donnas and big egos. That's not who they are. Real A-Players aren't strutting around like they own the place. They're in the trenches, just like you. They're humble. They're focused. They don't fear hard work. **They know how to effectively communicate, delegate, and coach their team.**

They're grounded. They're gritty. And they care about the work, the customers, and the people beside them. These are the ones who bleed the team's values, chase your purpose because it's their core purpose too, and strive daily for excellence, 1% better every single day. And they call out bad behaviour.

Here's what I know from decades of working with family businesses and entrepreneurial teams: High performers don't just generate results. They reduce stress. They lift standards. They save time, protect profit, and drive cashflow. But only if they are led well, understand exactly what winning looks like, and are held accountable to it. That's your job as their leader.

If someone needs babysitting, applause, or constant ego-stroking? That's not an A-Player. And to be honest, I never have the time or patience for any team member who isn't prepared to give themselves and the business their personal best. **I love creating a culture and environment where everyone can deliver their life's best work. Because in my**

opinion, everyone wants to succeed. Everyone wants to be someone, and as a leader and caretaker of their careers, you can support them and bring their dreams to life.

Now, let me translate that into something every business owner understands, cash.

A-Players generate momentum. They get things done without being micromanaged. They don't dodge responsibility or create internal friction. Instead, they create value. They think ahead. Period. They see around corners, and when your business moves faster, with fewer mistakes and reworks, less drama, and better outcomes, your cash conversion cycle starts to sing. You earn more. You waste less. You can afford to reward and celebrate with them too. *That* is very powerful and will be part of your legacy.

Getting the right people on the bus

So, how do you build your team of A-Players?

Adopt the Topgrading mindset

Start by embracing the philosophy that settling is expensive. The cost of a poor hire is more than just salary; it's wasted time, team morale, lost revenue, and missed opportunity.

You're not looking for someone good enough. You're looking for *the top 10% performers for the role, at your pay, in your context.*

Build scorecards that clarify excellence

Each role in your business should have a scorecard that's simple, clear, and measurable. What are the top 3-5 accountabilities? What metrics define success? If someone walked into the role today, how would they know if they were excelling?

When A-Players have crystal clarity on their KPIs and outcomes, they thrive. When they're guessing with vague expectations, they leave or, worse, disengage.

Coach, don't babysit

You don't need to micromanage A-Players; you do need to coach them. Coaching isn't rescuing. It's removing roadblocks, providing feedback, and holding space for performance. It's about making expectations visible and checking in regularly.

If you want to attract and keep A-Players, you have to become a great coach, not just a stressed-out boss barking orders. That never ends well.

Fire fast, hire slow

Hanging on to underperformers is one of the fastest ways to kill momentum and drain your cash. Every month that you delay making a decision costs you hard earned, precious cash. Be clear, be kind, but be decisive. That empty seat costs less than the wrong butt in it.

When hiring, slow it down. Use structured interviews. Ask candidates for examples of past outcomes, not vague strengths. Run reference checks that dig deep. Look for patterns, not promises.

At the end of the day, your business isn't just measured in Gross Margin Dollars and metrics, it's felt. By your team. By your customers. By you. A-Players don't just deliver results, they awaken trust, confidence, and calm. They're the ones who turn chaos into clarity, pressure into progress, and tension into invigorating teamwork.

And that's the real power move: Building a business that feels as good as it performs. As the saying goes, *"People will forget what you said, people will forget what you did, but people will never forget how you made them feel."*

That's what A-Players bring. And when your team leaves people feeling seen, respected, and relieved that they chose to work with your business? That's when the cash starts to follow.

Culture becomes magnetic. Results compound. Clients notice. You sleep better.

And that bank account? It finally starts acting like the reward it was always meant to be.

Because mediocrity is expensive and excellence is addictive.

You want a kickass cashflow? Then you need a kickass team. Period.

Bonus tip

Any team that isn't relying on external expertise or strategic facilitators is, by definition, underperforming. Just as the best swimmers, tennis players, and football teams all have an outside expert coach sharing their insights on how to achieve top performance, so too must your leadership team. As tempting as it is to try and do it all yourself, there is a significant advantage to bringing a fresh set of eyes into the leadership team meetings. As an external strategic facilitator, I have often found $1m on a Post-it note that has been stuck up on the wall by a team member. Experienced external advisers have no bias, no back story, and a lens focused purely on the goal that the company's cashflow must always win. We hear and see ideas and conversations from a different perspective. And quite often it's sifting through the avalanche of ideas and conversations to see how initiatives will help cashflow improve.

Kickass Cashflow Power Move #22

Hire powerhouses who believe in what you believe. No more babysitting. And invite an external strategic facilitator to run your meetings. I promise the cash ROI is insane!

To watch a video of Anna explaining the definition of an A-Player go to: **www.KickassCashflow.com**

"Teamwork makes the dream work, but a vision becomes a nightmare when the leader has a big dream and a bad team."

— John C. Maxwell

DAY 23

Your Finance Dream Team

Your tax and finance team are like podiatrists, holding a pedometer, watching how many steps you took. Your CFO, in contrast, is like an optometrist who helps you focus on what's ahead and where you're going.

Different skills. Different perspectives. Different value.

You need both. And when they work together, magic happens.

I often use this analogy when I keynote. In today's fast-paced business environment, it's not enough for your finance team to simply keep the books in order. They need to be forward-focused, commercially aware, and brave enough to have the tough conversations. The best ones don't just close the books; they also provide a clear view on your possible future.

A great finance team is proactive. They don't sit back and wait for the month to end. They're constantly scanning the horizon, identifying risks before they become problems and making recommendations that protect and propel your cashflow.

I agree with Scaling Up founder and CEO Verne Harnish, who wrote the foreword to this book, that the first hire a fast-growing company *must* make is a badass accounting team. And if you can afford one, a seasoned CFO is a great asset to tap into.

The job of a great finance team

I've sat in countless boardrooms and strategically facilitated high-growth teams. When we have a competent, collaborative CFO, the game seriously lifts.

Here's what a great finance team looks like in action: they sit down once a week and give you a clear, current view of your cashflow. But they don't stop there, they bring recommendations for improvement.

They're incorporating sales forecasts, not just expenses. They understand how payment terms and customer behaviour impacts the timing of cash. They track what's coming in, what's going out, and where things might get tight. And they're not afraid to say, "Hey, we need to hold off on that spend" or "It's time to chase that big invoice".

Weekly finance updates, when done well, create confidence. They give you visibility. And they make sure no one's flying blind.

Regular meetings between the sales and finance teams are crucial. This collaboration ensures that sales teams aren't just chasing deals, willy-nilly. They understand the *timing* of deals and how they affect cash (see Day 2).

Where there's confusion: All accountants are not equal

Not all accountants do the same job. And not all of them think the same way. Let's break down how it works:

The bookkeeper

These are your bill-paying, money-receiving, accounts payable, accounts receivable, and bookkeeping rockstars. They're the ones who touch every transaction, every day. They're involved in the details, making sure suppliers get paid on time, there's follow-up when customers' invoices are overdue, and your team gets their payslips without a hitch.

The best bookkeepers don't just enter data; they allocate correctly so that your reports are match-fit for decision-making.

The payroll manager

Your payroll manager is the person who holds the trust of your whole team. Get payroll wrong, and confidence erodes fast. Get it right, and this individual is the silent hero of the business.

The tax agent in "compliance"

Every business owner knows this detail-obsessed expert, who discovers every tax deduction, tracks your assets, and calculates your tax. Their job is accuracy and compliance. They're not built to forecast; they're wired to protect you. And when they're good, they're worth their weight in gold.

The CFO and their team

This is your future-focused team. They ask, "Where are we going? What will it take to get there?" They're not interested in the minutiae; they're focused on scenarios, projections, and growth decisions.

If your business is big enough (typically revenue greater than $20m), then your CFO should be your commercial co-pilot. They help with strategy, leases, equipment purchases, pricing decisions. They answer your "what if?" questions. And they challenge assumptions, so you don't get caught in wishful thinking.

A great CFO also unlocks your sales potential. They know which customers and services are most profitable. Smart sales teams love them because they show where the biggest wins are hiding.

But here's the thing: *A CFO can only make smart decisions with accurate data*. They're relying on the integrity of the numbers your internal finance team has entered. If your books are messy or slow to update, you're flying blind. A brilliant CFO backed by a sloppy accounting team is like a race car driver with a spluttering motor and foggy windshield. Visibility matters. Speed matters. Precision matters.

The management accountant

Somewhere between your compliance team and your CFO lives another critical role: the management accountant. These folks are the bridge. They dig into the data, analyse trends, and deliver reports that inform day-to-day decisions. They're tactical, curious, and fluent in both past performance and future planning.

A great management accountant isn't just churning out monthly reports, they're spotting cost blowouts, tracking Gross Margin Dollars, and helping department heads stay on track. They play a vital role in budgeting, forecasting, and monitoring performance. They give you the signal when something's going off-course so you can course correct early.

Different skills, distinctive psychology

Most people don't realise that tax agents, internal accountants, and CFOs have completely different psychologies.

Tax agents and bookkeepers are past-focused. They care about accuracy to the decimal. And while that can be frustrating when you're trying to move quickly, their precision protects you.

CFOs, in contrast, are comfortable with ambiguity. They're estimating, forecasting, and scenario-planning in big numbers. They think ahead, not in retrospect.

Trying to find one person who does both? Rare. Unicorn-level rare. They do exist, but you'll usually get a much better result by building a team with complementary strengths.

The bottom line: All accountants are not equal. If you want a business with strong financial health, you need a finance team that covers the past, the present, and the future.

That's a lot of finance horsepower and way too expensive for any family business to access, and that's why I created the Kickass Cashflow Cashinator's Checklist. The checklist is a set of cashflow habits practiced by high-growth companies. It's a simple list of best practices designed to keep profit protected and cash flowing. We'll cover this more in the next chapter.

Kickass Cashflow Power Move #23

Put the right people in the right seats on your finance team.

"If we did all the things we are capable of doing, we would literally astound ourselves."

— Thomas A. Edison

DAY 24

The Kickass Cashflow Cashinator™

Meet your Cashinator

Most small- and medium-sized businesses can't afford the luxury of a big-city accounting department. You don't have a CFO number-crunching your strategy at one end or a team of analysts pumping out dashboards at the other. What you usually have is a bookkeeper keeping the basics in order and an accountant who swoops in once a year for tax. That leaves a massive gap, right where the daily cashflow decisions are made.

And those decisions matter. They fuel confident action, because nothing burns cash faster than procrastination due to missing or late information. Cashflow clarity determines whether you lead with confidence or second-guess every move, whether reports arrive in time to act or too late to matter.

That's why I created the **Cashinator** role: the missing link between the high-end CFO and the hands-on bookkeeping team. Someone who protects your profit, powers your cashflow, and gives you the clarity you need to lead with confidence.

If you want steady profits, consistent cashflow, and fewer nights worrying about payroll (or whether you can finally book that cruise) you need this one role in your business.

Meet your new BFF: The Cashinator

Every Business owner needs a Cashinator whispering "margin" in one ear and "cashflow" in the other. They're your wingman, your good angel on the shoulder, the steady voice in your head reminding you to protect margin, stick to terms, and make decisions that keep cash flowing. Quietly but powerfully, they transform how your business runs. And yes, with a Cashinator by your side, you'll finally sleep better at night.

Most businesses don't struggle because they can't sell. They struggle because they don't understand and manage their cashflow decisions.

On the surface, everything looks fine, the orders are coming in, the team is busy, the numbers are climbing. But underneath? Margins are too thin, discounts slide through unchecked, commissions chew into profit, payment terms stretch too far, and overdue invoices pile up.

That's not a sales problem. That's a cashflow problem. And it's exactly where hard work and cash quietly vaporise.

The Cashinator stops the leaks. Their job is to make sure every deal adds value, and every invoice turns into cash in the bank.

Here's how they do it. They

- check margins before quotes go out,
- chase payments fast,
- enforce trading terms that protect you,
- flag risky deals before approval,
- send accurate invoices on time,
- teach the team how margin and cash connect, and
- build simple processes and systems everyone can follow to ensure that cash is collected and spent efficiently.

This isn't about micromanagement. It's about clarity, consistency, and building a rhythm where cashflow decisions fuel growth instead of draining it.

The Cashinator makes sure processes are in place to ensure deposits are taken upfront, every single time. That terms are short and clear, and late payments are followed up immediately. They set up meetings, record and monitor action items, and make sure all promises are kept. They facilitate updating the rolling cashflow forecast, keep the sales team focused and accountable, and ensure that every cashflow decision, from quoting to collecting, strengthens your bank balance.

At Performance 7, Nathan is our Cashinator. He checks every deal, keeps proposals sharp, and monitors job profitability. Nathan is super focused on keeping an eye on every client engagement to make sure the clients are happy and that the engagements are within scope. That clarity means we can quote with confidence, know when to walk away, and protect our cashflow without regret.

Cashinators design the fireproof processes and systems that keep your cashflow steady.

This is how you build a business that lasts

Appoint your Cashinator. Give them authority, access to the numbers, and visibility across teams. Look for emotional intelligence, sharp questioning, and the ability to think ahead.

When this role is taken seriously, here's what happens:

- Margins sing.
- Bank balances rise.
- The team understands the impact of their decisions.
- You shift from reacting to leading with control and being proactive.
- You stop leaking profit on deals that only look good on paper.
- You stop waiting months for money that should already be yours.
- You stop working harder for less and start leading smarter for more.

Your next steps

- ☐ Appoint your Cashinator.
- ☐ Protect your margin.
- ☐ Stand firm on your terms.
- ☐ Map your processes.
- ☐ Build your systems.
- ☐ Own your cashflow like a boss.

The sooner you embrace this role, the sooner you'll lead with clarity. That's how you build a business that doesn't just grow but it kicks ass!

Kickass Cashflow Power Move #24

Decide who will be your Cashinator. Start ticking off that Kickass Cashflow Checklist.

"The secret of getting ahead is getting started. The secret of getting started is breaking your complex, overwhelming tasks into small, manageable tasks and then starting on the first one."

— Mark Twain

DAY 25

Your Kickass Cashflow Checklist

The **Kickass Cashflow Checklist** is about the small, consistent habits you repeat every day. This checklist keeps those habits front and centre. It's simple, it's practical, and it works. When your business runs on a proven set of cashflow habits, you protect profit, keep money moving, and make decisions with clarity. And that's how steady habits turn into steady cashflow.

Read through the Kickass Cashflow Checklist, tick off what you already have in place, and highlight one habit that you'll commit to next. Every tick and highlight is a step toward stronger cashflow.

Let's go!

Kickass Cashflow: Your checklist to cashflow excellence

1. Grow the Jaws of Margin Dollars to scale your business

- ☐ The team understands the true power of pricing and its relationship with discounting and volume.
- ☐ Each member of the sales team has clear Gross Margin Dollar targets, per month, per quarter, and per year.
- ☐ Product and/or job profitability is tracked and reviewed weekly. Non-profitable products or service lines are eliminated.
- ☐ There is a person accountable for growing Gross Margin Dollars.

2. The marketing team exists to generate profitable, qualified leads

- ☐ Marketing knows the core customer and their Gross Margin Dollars contribution.
- ☐ Marketing tracks customer acquisition costs (CAC) at least monthly.
- ☐ Marketing continually tests and evolves an exhilarating value proposition for your core customer(s).
- ☐ The lifetime value of a customer must be greater than the customer acquisition costs.

3. Sales teams and sales cycles are highly efficient

- ☐ Every salesperson has leading KPIs that directly link back to the rolling cashflow forecast.
- ☐ Sales teams have at least two daily huddles; one for rehearsals, tactic building, and moral support, the other for outcomes.
- ☐ The sales process is clear and visible, and the probability of closing is tracked weekly.

- ☐ Every salesperson understands the difference between margin and markup.

4. Cost of goods sold (COGS) is optimised

- ☐ The operations team is clear on the cost of goods/units and meets weekly to improve without compromising quality and speed.
- ☐ Stock holdings: Inventory turns and/or work in progress are tracked and optimised.
- ☐ All rebates, supplier agreements, freight, and exchange rate costs are reviewed at least monthly.
- ☐ Project profitability is tracked weekly, and disbursements and receipts are collected easily.

5. Eliminate or minimise accounts receivable

- ☐ Review your payment terms to collect customer payments faster.
- ☐ Receive a deposit for at least the cost of your goods, or wages, before you commit resources.
- ☐ The sales team agrees on payment terms during the sales process.
- ☐ You reconcile accounts receivable daily and chase up weekly.

6. Everyone understands the true cashflow impact of a new hire

- ☐ All oncosts are included when calculating the new hire.
- ☐ The leadership team understands the difference in revenue and/or Gross Margin Dollars needed to hire additional revenue-generating labour.
- ☐ The leadership team understands the difference in revenue and/or Gross Margin Dollars needed to hire additional non-revenue-generating labour.
- ☐ Customer payment trading terms should be shorter than payroll cycles.

7. Your finance team provides weekly recommendations to make cashflow improvements

- ☐ Weekly cashflows are updated to adjust for the sales team's forecast.
- ☐ Profitability vs. cash contribution by customer, product, and market segment are presented as waterfall graphs.
- ☐ Your finance team provides weekly recommendations to make cashflow improvements.
- ☐ The go-to-market team and finance team work together to create sales forecasts.

8. Conduct a financial health check monthly

- ☐ Conduct an expense audit monthly.
- ☐ Eliminate family expenses to normalise the business's performance.
- ☐ To get a true picture of the business's performance, pay or adjust the reports to reflect family members' true market salaries.
- ☐ Keep a separate bank account for your tax obligations.

9. Build your cashflow runway

- ☐ Create an efficient scaling machine by measuring the ultimate metric: cashflow.
- ☐ Monitor Gross Margin Dollars per full-time employee.
- ☐ Create products and services that encourage repeat purchases for existing customers.
- ☐ Create maintenance contracts or subscriptions to even out your cashflow.

10. All employees understand the impact of their decisions on the business's cashflow

- ☐ Everyone participates in financial training and understands the difference between profit, cash, and cashflow.
- ☐ All teams participate in a quarterly Power of One workshop(s).
- ☐ All teams participate in a quarterly cash conversion cycle workshop(s).
- ☐ All teams can read the financials, and their questions are answered.

Kickass Cashflow Power Move #25

Work through this checklist with your leadership team and decide which habit to focus on improving this month.

"Very few people ever made a great idea come to life without a lot of help."

— Sir Richard Branson

DAY 26

Your X-Factor

Imagine if your whole team showed up the way Beyoncé envisions it: Bold, clear, and unapologetically determined to succeed. That kind of vibe? It's not just empowering; it's the secret sauce to *cashflow greatness.*

Here's the truth: When your *finance team* and your *go-to-market crew* (sales and marketing) are in sync, magic happens. Not the fluffy unicorn kind; the real, bank account–boosting kind.

Sales and marketing are out there living in the wild, tracking buyer behaviour, watching market shifts, riding the energy. Meanwhile, finance is decoding all that chaos into forecasts, Gross Margin Dollars, and cashflow timing.

One side holds the story.

The other holds the scoreboard.

But you only win when they play on the same team.

Too many businesses treat these departments like they're living on opposite planets, sales chasing numbers like they're sprinting through a jungle, and finance clutching their spreadsheets like they're guarding the Holy Grail.

But in high-performance businesses? These teams are *joined at the hip*. Like Beyoncé and her mic, inseparable and unstoppable.

When they collaborate, you get forecasts that aren't just hopeful, they're accurate. No more playing cashflow roulette. You're operating with clarity, not chaos.

But don't kid yourself, this doesn't just happen. It takes rhythm and discipline:

- Weekly or fortnightly check-ins between sales and finance leaders (yes, put it in the calendar and don't ghost it)
- Real-time updates on pipeline shifts, deal timing, and payment expectations
- Shared agreement on what's coming in and when, so you don't commit to spending money that hasn't landed yet

When this system hums, decision-making flips from reactive to strategic. You're not squinting into the future; you're scanning it with a telescope.

You start spotting cash spikes before they surge and droughts before they dry you out. You know when to push hard, when to hold back, and when to straight-up walk away. Sales starts closing cleaner, more profitable deals. Finance stops getting blindsided. Everyone breathes easier. **Communication and collaboration is your X-factor.**

And the result?

Better forecasting.

Stronger Gross Margin Dollars.

A business that runs with *intention*, not just *intensity.*

Here's a little pro-tip that A-Player salespeople know: *The finance team is not the fun police; they're their best friend. They're a secret weapon.*

Your accounting team knows exactly where the fat Gross Margin Dollars hide, which clients pay like clockwork, and where your real money-makers are. Want to sell smarter? Ask accounting.

If you're running an established business, guess what? You're already sitting on a *treasure trove* of financial data. It's in your accounting software just waiting to be mined. Customer patterns, real cost to serve, and payment cycles. It's all there, and it's wildly underutilised.

Don't let that gold gather dust. Leverage it. Turn that data into your unfair advantage.

Because when your story and your numbers are in harmony, you stop chasing cashflow.

You create it.

Kickass Cashflow Power Move #26

Set up regular, dedicated talk time for your go-to-market and finance team.

SECTION 6

Let's Turn On Those High Beams

Rolling Cashflow Forecast

Rapid Fire Shots

KPIs That Move the Needle: Why Scorecards and Dashboards Are Your Cashflow's Best Friend

There's a reason your eyes are at the front of your head: You're built to move forward. Business is no different. You're here to lead, to build, to grow. But you can't do that if you're blind to what's ahead. Yet most business owners are driving their business in the dark, with no lights on, let alone their high beams. They can't "see" what's ahead. Sure, you have a budget… but when has that ever been right? Budgets are stagnant. Rolling cashflows are alive, just like your business.

If you've ever driven at dusk as the light fades, you know the feeling. That tension in your chest. The instinct to slow down. The sudden panic when something appears on the road too late to react. That's exactly what running a business without a cashflow forecast feels like. You're reacting instead of leading. Hoping instead of planning. Bracing instead of building.

It's time to turn the lights on.

This section is all about the importance of building your cashflow forecasting muscle. Not just to survive but to design your future with clarity and control. Because when you can see what's coming, you can make smarter decisions, seize opportunities, and avoid the potholes that take others out.

A rolling cashflow forecast is life changing.

"No pilot will take off without knowing if they have enough fuel to land safely at their destination. How on earth can any business owner run their business without knowing if they have enough cash to fuel their growth?"

— Richard de Crespigny AM, Pilot in Command QF32

DAY 27

Rolling Cashflow Forecast

Every business idea looks fantastic on a spreadsheet

A few formulas, a sprinkle of optimism, and suddenly you're scaling to the moon in 12 months flat. Cute. But if it looks *too* good? You're probably missing something… big.

Spreadsheets are magical liars. They behave perfectly until it's time for your team to deliver on the fantasy you built in Excel.

Don't stop at the budget. Budgeting alone is like buying a gym membership and thinking you'll get fit just by owning the card. Your 90-day plan needs more muscle. That's where your rolling cashflow forecast steps in; it's the behind-the-scenes badass that keeps your business solvent and your stress levels out of the red.

Yes, it takes more effort. Yes, it's one more thing. But trust me: *the clarity, confidence, and control* you'll gain? Worth it.

Budget vs. Cashflow: Know the difference

Let's clear this up. *A budget is your best guess* at revenue and expenses over a set period, usually a year. It's helpful, sure. But it's static. It tells you how profitable you *might* be… eventually. And the one thing you can guarantee about the budget is that it will be 100% wrong when it goes live.

Cashflow, on the other hand, is all about timing. When is the money coming in? When is it going *out*? Because, spoiler: The bills don't care if your annual budget says you'll have money in October. They're due *now*.

Here's where a lot of businesses get blindsided. Your budget says you're going to crush it, and there are high-fives all around. But if your clients are slow to pay or you've overcommitted your spending? You could be staring down a cash crunch with zero warning.

So, your finance team's real job? Ditch the budget and spend the time on updating 90-day rolling cashflow forecasts every Friday. This way, you'll get real-time intel to guide smart decisions fast. Even better, ask your leadership team to sign off on the forecast so that they can commit to the numbers. This way, they're not abdicating their accuracy to the finance team. They're active participants in the cashflow forecasting process, and you can rely on them.

A finance team that's in the game

Your finance team shouldn't be sitting on the sidelines, buried in spreadsheets, only emerging to say "no" to new expenses. They should be upfront, calling plays with your sales, ops, and leadership teams.

They're not just reporting numbers, they're surfacing insights like

- which products and customers bring in cash (not just paper profits),
- where your Jaws of Margin are squeezing, and
- what risks are around the corner based on how your pipeline is moving.

When finance, sales, and ops are meeting regularly, you stop reacting. You start *predicting*. And that's when you go from survival mode to strategic leadership.

Real cash confidence comes from rhythm

Want to build cashflow confidence into your culture? Create a rhythm:

- *Weekly or fortnightly syncs* between the finance and GTM teams
- *Pipeline updates* that include likely close dates and payment timing
- *Cash-based reforecasting* tied to real-time decisions (not old assumptions)
- *Sign-offs* that we're good to go

This is how you catch cash potholes before you fall into them. It's how you know when to say yes to growth opportunities or when to slam the brakes.

When you've got this rhythm, you stop flying blind. You can see your cash runway, your hidden risks, and your upside all at once.

Bottom line? Rolling cashflow forecasting isn't a "nice to have"; it's your business's early-warning system, growth enabler, and peace-of-mind machine all rolled into one.

Get on top of it, and you won't just survive, you'll scale with swagger.

For a free worksheet to start building your rolling cashflow forecast go to: **www.KickassCashflow.com**

Kickass Cashflow Power Move #27

Fill in the spreadsheet on the following page (Figure 9) and build your rolling cashflow forecast.

90 Day Rolling Cashflow Forecasting Template – Example

	P&L Forecast	Quarter / 90 Days		
		Month 1	Month 2	Month 3
		Forecast	Forecast	Forecast
Step 1	**Sales** Number of customers Av sale per customer **Total Sales** Cost of Sales – merchant fees			
	Gross profit	$ -	$ -	$ -
	Overheads			
	Total Expenditure	$ -	$ -	$ -
	NET Profit	$ -	$ -	$ -

	Cash Flow Forecast	Quarter / 90 Days		
		Month 1	Month 2	Month 3
		Forecast	Forecast	Forecast
Step 2	**Opening Bank Balance**	$ -	$ -	$ -
	Cash Inflows Cash received from Customer Sales			
	Total Cash inflows	$ -	$ -	$ -
	Cash Outflows Cost of Sales Salary & Wages Super Public Liability Insurances Insurances Operational Expenses Team Amenities Rent Motor Vehicle Repayments Contractors GST PAYG Other			
	Total Cash Outflows	$ -	$ -	$ -
	Closing Bank Balance	$ -	$ -	$ -

Figure 9: Rolling Cashflow Forecast

"It's never the one big thing, the one magic and lucky moment. It all comes down to a relentless series of 1% excellence moves, that eventually breaks down the competition."

— Craig Bellamy, one of the greatest modern-day coaches in any sport

DAY 28

Rapid Fire Shots

Ready to clean up your numbers, slash the fluff, and unlock your next level of cashflow?

This chapter will hit you with truth bombs, one after the other.

Stop dabbling; get serious about cash

You don't build cashflow confidence by luck. You build it through visibility, sharp decision-making, and clean-as-a-whistle numbers. This isn't about penny-pinching or pretending tax bills don't exist. It's about treating your financials like the strategic weapon they are.

The eight-phone nightmare and other wild discoveries

One of my clients was paying for *eight phone bills* for team members who hadn't worked there in over a year. Why? Everyone assumed someone else was handling it. The accountants thought ops had cancelled it. Ops thought HR had flagged it. HR thought finance was on it. You already know where this is going.

Meanwhile, the business was leaking thousands a year.

Every dollar matters (but cutting costs alone won't ever save you)

Yes, review your general ledger. Yes, slash waste. But no, cutting costs to the bone is not a growth strategy; it's survival mode. You can't save your way to success. True profitability comes from clarity, pricing, margin discipline, and knowing exactly where every dollar goes and why.

Action: Here's what to do (right now)

- ☐ **Print your general ledger every quarter:** Go line-by-line. Be brutal.
- ☐ **Train your team:** Get them cost-aware.
- ☐ **Create clear policies:** For travel, entertainment, subscriptions, and supplier spend.
- ☐ **Reward smart savings:** People love recognition, make it part of your culture.
- ☐ **Review your suppliers:** Renegotiate, consolidate, and shop around.
- ☐ **Ask for rebates:** So much cash gets left on the table because no one asks.

Every clean cut = cash back in the bank

Every dollar you reclaim is a dollar you can reinvest into better tools, smarter people, or simply breathe easier knowing your cash runway just got longer.

Bonus round: Seven fast truth bombs that will change your game

Before owner's theft (BOT)

All those little "personal" expenses? The groceries, the holidays, the Spotify account? Stop. You're not clever. You're clouding your numbers and hurting your ability to make smart decisions. Clean them out.

Cashflow impact: Personal fluff inflates your expenses and messes with profit. Cut it out, get clean, and start seeing clearly.

Pay yourself a real wage

Underpaying yourself doesn't make you a hero. It makes your numbers lie. If you can't replace yourself with the wage you take, you don't have a business – you have a fantasy.

Cashflow impact: Normalise wages. Real costs = real decisions = real business.

Separate your tax obligations

That GST money? Not yours. That PAYG? Also not yours. Stop pretending you're richer than you are. Set up a second bank account and move that money the minute it lands.

Cashflow impact: No surprises. No panic. Just smooth, stress-free compliance.

Lazy cash? Time to give it a job

You know that stash sitting around doing nothing while you hustle? That cash could be working for you. Whether it's earning interest, backing growth, or cushioning risk, lazy cash needs a purpose.

Cashflow impact: Place this cash in interest bearing accounts, whilst you figure out where to invest next.

Build a cash cushion

On the flip side, *no cash cushion*? That's a gamble. You can't pounce on opportunities or weather surprises without quick access to funds. So be smart. Build a plan for *both* your surplus and your shortfalls.

Cashflow impact: You're prepared for all opportunities.

Your reports are lying to you

Feel-good P&Ls with made-up wages, personal expenses, and "soft" forecasting? Garbage. Rip off the rose-tinted glasses. Demand reports that reflect *actual* performance.

Cashflow impact: Real numbers = confident decisions = scalable business.

How much cash should you hold?

Here's the deal:

- **Stable, recurring revenue?** You can keep a leaner buffer, perhaps 3-6 months.
- **Unpredictable, seasonal, or project-based?** You need more reserves, 6-9 months.

In *Good to Great*, Jim Collins found that the best companies had *10x the cash reserves* of their peers. They weren't luckier. They were battle ready.

Cashflow impact: Cash lets you seize opportunity, not scramble for survival.

Final action list: Build your cashflow fortress

- [ ] Print your general ledger every quarter. Review with leadership.
- [ ] Set up a tax bucket account. Transfer GST and PAYG fortnightly.
- [ ] Open a separate investment account. Save before you spend. Normalise wages, both yours and your team's.
- [ ] Clean personal expenses from your P&L. All of them.
- [ ] Renegotiate supplior deals and chase rebates.
- [ ] Train your ops team to be cost-conscious and cash-smart.
- [ ] Conduct monthly expense audits.
- [ ] Remove software, tech, or tools that aren't pulling their weight.
- [ ] Keep 3-6 months' cash reserves based on sales stability.

Cash at bank is the only number that doesn't lie

Set up the systems. Build the reports. Clean the mess. And give yourself the confidence of *knowing*, not guessing where your money is, where it's going, and what it's earning you in return.

Because *in a world full of variables, cash is your truth.*

Kickass Cashflow Power Move #28

Know how much true cash in the bank you have every day.

From a kitchen table near you…
“In the absence of real numbers, data, and facts, let’s all agree to go with my emotional opinion.”

— Anon

DAY 29

KPIs That Move the Needle: Why Scorecards and Dashboards Are Your Cashflow's Best Friend

When I walk into a family business that's stuck, stressed, or struggling to hit its targets, I can almost guarantee one thing: Their team is flying blind. No dashboards. No scorecards. No clear link between what the team does every week and what's happening in the bank account. They might be working hard, but they're not working smart.

That's where job scorecards and KPIs come in. Not just as fluffy HR tools, but as the steering wheel of your cashflow strategy. When used properly, KPIs create a direct and measurable link between your team's daily actions and your 90-day rolling cashflow forecast. This chapter is your practical roadmap to build that bridge, one metric at a time.

Why KPIs are the beating heart of cashflow strategy

KPIs are not just about performance reviews or ticking boxes. The right KPIs, reviewed in the right rhythm, help you *control* your cashflow weeks before something hits the P&L.

Think of your business as a car. Your cashflow forecast is the GPS. Your KPIs are the dashboard dials telling you whether you're accelerating toward your goals or about to break down on the side of the road.

Unfortunately, most businesses only look at the rearview mirror. They obsess over *lagging indicators* like revenue, profit, or cash on hand. These are important, but they're *outcomes*. By the time you see them, it's already too late to change course.

That's where *leading KPIs* become your best friend. These are the early signs that they measure the activity metrics that predict cashflow, not just reflect it.

The best way to explain the difference between leading and lagging KPIs is that your calorie intake and number of steps are leading KPIs and your weight is your lagging KPI. If you track the inputs, you will deliver the results.

So, whilst many of us stare at the accountant's reports, you are only analysing history. I encourage you to find ways to track and incentivise activities (leading KPIs) that will deliver the results you want.

Scorecards, dashboards, and a 90-day cashflow forecast that talks

This rolling forecast is updated every Friday. And guess what? Your KPIs are the drivers behind every row.

For example,

- the sales forecast depends on how many qualified leads were generated this week,
- debtor receipts are driven by follow-up activity on overdue invoices, and
- supplier payments link directly to project completion KPIs.

The leading KPI metrics dashboard

Now let's get to the juicy part: The real-time metrics that *predict* whether that forecast will hold up.

Table 7 shows a snapshot of what a weekly executive KPI dashboard might look like.

Metric	Target	This Week	Trend vs. Last Week
Qualified Leads Generated	25	22	⬆ +2
Sales Calls Made	50	48	⬇ –4
Quote Follow-Ups Sent	40	35	➡ 0
Debtors Overdue ($)	<10k	$8,500	⬇ –$1,000
Projects Completed & Invoiced	10	12	⬆ +2
Team Utilisation Rate (%)	85%	87%	⬆ +4%

Table 7: Weekly executive KPI dashboard

Each of these KPIs *maps directly* to a part of the cashflow forecast.

Job scorecard example: sales leader

Let's say Sarah is your sales manager. Her scorecard might look like Table 8.

Role Objective	KPI	Target	Rhythm
Grow margin dollars by increasing the sales pipeline	New qualified leads per week	25	Weekly
Convert leads to proposals	Proposals sent	20	Weekly
Drive margin predictability	Pipeline-to-sale conversion rate	30%+	Weekly
Accelerate cash collection	Proposal to invoice days	<14 days	Weekly

Table 8: Example dashboard for a sales manager

Now here's the magic: Sarah's weekly scorecard is reviewed alongside the KPI dashboard in the *executive team meeting*, and the results are used to update the 90-day forecast.

Leading vs. Lagging KPIs (and why it matters)

Lagging KPIs tell you *what happened*:

- Total revenue
- Gross margin
- Net profit
- Cash on hand

They're like checking your weight *after* three months of dieting. Good to know, but you can't change the past.

Leading KPIs tell you *what's about to happen*:

- Number of discovery calls booked
- Time to quote from the first enquiry
- Conversion rate this week
- AR follow-up calls made

These are the habits and actions that *create* the outcomes.

If you're only looking at lagging KPIs, you're running your business like a detective. You investigate problems after they've already hurt your bank account. But if you focus on leading KPIs, you run your business like a pilot navigating early, adjusting mid-flight, and staying cash positive.

Why this changes everything

If you want predictable cashflow, you need disciplined behaviour.

The only way to achieve that is to:

- set clear expectations through scorecards,
- measure what matters through leading KPIs, and
- link it all back to your 90-day rolling forecast.

> **BUSINESS OWNER'S TIP:**
> A mistake I see many business owners make is that their KPIs never link back to their cashflow forecast. Even more dangerous is that the KPIs are linked to a budget which is way past its used date and no longer relevant. I can't stress this enough. Your business is *alive,* and so are your forecasts and KPIs. Bring them to life and set your team and your business up for success. This is especially true if your business is fast-growing.

When a team member can say, "If I hit this metric, we'll close X more deals, which means $50k more in July," that's power. That's clarity. That's real-time leadership that builds momentum instead of reacting to crises.

Let's stop managing cashflow in hindsight. Your team's scorecards and KPIs are the front line strategy for cash confidence. Now go build the dashboard, run the meeting, and lead like you *mean* it.

Kickass Cashflow Power Move #29

Make sure your KPIs drive behaviour that delivers your cashflow forecast.

"In five seconds flat, you made, what I call, a 'heart-first' decision. You ignore your fears and let your courage and confidence speak for you. Five seconds of courage makes all the difference."

– Mel Robbins

SECTION 7

It's Time to Kickass Your Cashflow

Close the Knowing-Doing Gap

"Education is worthless, unless you implement."

— Anna Samios

DAY 30

Close the Knowing-Doing Gap

What's next? Let's make it happen!

So here you are at the end of the book, and **hopefully at the beginning of something bigger**.

If you've made it this far, then one thing's already crystal clear: **You care deeply about your business**.

You're not here to coast. You're not content with "just getting by". You want a business that thrives, one that fuels your vision, supports your people, and leaves a little something extra in the bank account.

And I want that for you too.

Writing this book has been a way to pass the mic to give business owners like you the tools, language, and confidence to stop being intimidated by numbers and start using them as your greatest asset. But I know reading a book is just the first step.

Sometimes, you need more. You need someone in your corner. Someone to walk beside you, push when needed, clarify when it's messy, and celebrate the wins that come from getting cashflow right.

Here's where we go from here

So, if you're fired up and thinking, *this is exactly what we need but I want help applying it to my business...*

I've got you.

You can work with me and my team in a few powerful ways:

Consulting for business owners ready to level up

If your financials feel like a black box or you've outgrown your systems, pricing, or cash habits, we'll help you unpack the mess and turn it into clarity and control. One-on-one. No fluff. Just real support for real businesses.

Jump on my online cashflow course

Prefer to learn at your own pace, on your own schedule? Then dive into the full Kickass Cashflow Masterclass through our self-paced course at: **www.KickassCashflow.com**

It's punchy, practical, and packed with real-world tools you can use straight away.

Public training workshops

We run live workshops for business owners and teams who want to go deeper into the cashflow strategies covered in this book. It's training with heart, brains, and bold outcomes, and you'll leave with your next steps mapped out.

Keynote speaking gigs

If you've got a conference, summit, or event full of entrepreneurs or business owners, I'd love to bring the energy. My keynotes are real, relatable, and deeply practical. No theory, no fluff. Just straight talk that sparks change.

Tailored in-house training

Want to bring this thinking into your business or leadership team? We can create a custom training session based on your specific challenges. Your team will walk away aligned, empowered, and equipped to drive performance through better numbers.

And lastly...

I truly hope this book has lightened your load even just a little. Running a business is **not for the faint-hearted**. You've taken risks, carried responsibility, and held the vision through the ups and downs.

This book is my way of saying: *You're not alone.*

And you're definitely not the only one who's ever stared at a bank account, a budget, or a P&L and thought, *what the hell is going on here?*

If I've helped you feel more confident, even just 5% more, in the way you handle cash, make decisions, or lead your team, then I consider this book a success.

Want to connect?

I'm a real human, and yes, you can absolutely reach out.

Whether it's to book something, ask a question, or just say hi, you're welcome to connect with me directly.

Email: anna@Performance7.global
Website: www.Performance7.global
LinkedIn: Anna Samios

Let's build better businesses together.

Now go.

Take what you've learned and use it.

Lead with clarity. Spend with confidence. Grow with purpose.

Because *cash isn't just a number; it's your power.*

And you, my friend, are just getting started.

Anna ❤

Kickass Cashflow Power Move #30

Don't struggle alone. Expert help will accelerate your progress.

Acknowledgements

Peter Samios, Andrew Banks, Verne Harnish, Paul & Sonia Stovell, Alan Miltz, Joss Milne, Greg Crabtree, Peter Cameron, Ashley Hayden, Melissa Anderson, Dean McAuley, Jenna Samios, Nathan Samios, Denise Papamichos, John Papamichos, Michelle Reynolds, Michelle Paans-Wilson, Jamie Miller, David Allen, Chloe Cameron, Elaine Pofeldt, and my maths teacher, Miss Kerry Taylor.

About the Author

Anna Samios is an internationally recognised, award-winning business coach and the Founder and CEO of Kickass Cashflow and Performance 7.

With more than three decades of experience, Anna has built her reputation as one of Australia's most trusted advisors to entrepreneurs and executives who are serious about growth. She has advised over 400 companies across industries ranging from ambitious start-ups and family-owned enterprises to publicly listed corporations. Her client list reads like a who's who of high-performance leadership: AFR Fast Growth CEOs, influential Chairs, and even Australia's Rich Listers have sought her out for her practical, no-nonsense insights on scaling with confidence and clarity.

Over the years, Anna has become a sought-after voice on the keynote circuit, regularly sharing the stage with Shark Tank's Andrew Banks and Glen Richards. Her presentations are known for being bold, practical, and energising, leaving audiences with both the mindset shift and the tangible tools needed to turn chaos into cashflow. Whether she's speaking to a room full of CEOs, family business owners, or emerging entrepreneurs, Anna's message is clear: you can have clarity, cashflow, and confidence if you're willing to embrace the numbers and lead with purpose.

Anna's expertise has been recognised at the highest levels. She has been featured on Channel 7, in Harper's Bazaar, and across numerous industry associations, chambers of commerce, and local government programs. The Australian Federal Government's Entrepreneurs Program has also engaged her to advise high-growth companies in sectors such as IT, cybersecurity, and professional services underscoring her reputation as a strategist who can cut through complexity and deliver measurable results.

Since founding Performance 7, Anna and her team have become the go-to advisors for scale-ups and fast-growth businesses across Australia. Collectively, they guide companies that now generate more than $1.8 billion in revenue a figure that continues to climb every day. Under her leadership, Performance 7 has developed a reputation for being more than just consultants; they are partners in transformation, trusted to help ambitious businesses move from surviving to thriving.

Beyond her business achievements, Anna contributes her expertise to the arts and education sector as a proud Board Director of the National Institute of Dramatic Art Foundation (NIDA). In this role, she champions creativity, leadership, and the vital role that storytelling plays in shaping culture and business alike.

www.ingramcontent.com/pod-product-compliance
Ingram Content Group UK Ltd.
Pitfield, Milton Keynes, MK11 3LW, UK
UKHW041636190726
13854UKWH00006B/2517